John H Lockwood

Coney Island

John H Lockwood

Coney Island

ISBN/EAN: 9783743323186

Manufactured in Europe, USA, Canada, Australia, Japa

Cover: Foto ©ninafisch / pixelio.de

Manufactured and distributed by brebook publishing software (www.brebook.com)

John H Lockwood

Coney Island

CONEY ISLAND.

AN ILLUSTRATED

 GUIDE TO THE SEA

With Official Time Tables

SEASON OF 1883.

CONTAINING AN ACCOUNT OF A RAMBLE ON THE BEACH
BY A PLEASURE PARTY, BESIDES VALUABLE
LOCAL INFORMATION.

PUBLISHED BY TRUAX & CO.,
OFFICE, No. 253 FULTON ST., BROOKLYN

T. DE T. TRUAX.   J. H. LOCKWOOD.

Entered according to Act of Congress, in the Office of the Librarian of Congress, at Washington, D. C., by TRUAX & Co.

CONTENTS.

Coney Island, descriptive..p. 5
Brooklyn Bridge (Poem)..p. 8
Depot at West Brighton, descriptive..p. 14
Camera Obscura, descriptive..p. 16
Græco-Roman Carrosselle..pp. 16, 61
Observatory, descriptive..pp. 18, 61
Brighton Pier & Navigation Co., descriptive....................................p. 22
Mrs. Vanderveer's Bathing Pavilion, descriptive..............................p. 22
Sea Beach Palace Hotel, descriptive..p. 26
Ocean Pavilion, descriptive..p. 30
Paul Bauer's, descriptive...p. 34
Vanderveer's Hotel, descriptive..p. 38
Seaside Aquarium, descriptive...p. 42
Seaside Home for Children, descriptive...p. 44
Brighton Railroad, descriptive...p. 46
Hotel Brighton, descriptive..p. 48
Brighton Beach Pharmacy, descriptive..p. 50
Brighton Silk Works..p. 52
Brighton Beach Bathing Pavilion, descriptive.................................p. 52
Bunnell's Museum...p. 54
Manhattan Beach, descriptive..p. 56
Bombardment of Alexandria, descriptive..p. 60
New York & Brooklyn Bridge, descriptive.......................................p. 63
Prospect Park & Coney Island Railroad Time Table.........................p. 64
New York & Sea Beach Railroad Time Table...................................p. 65
    "   "   "   "   " Brooklyn Division.........p. 67
Brooklyn, Bath & Coney Island Railroad Time Table........................p. 69
Brooklyn, Flatbush & Coney Island R. R. Time Table (Flatbush Div.)...p. 71
    "   "   "   "   "   " (Bedford "...p. 73
    "   "   "   "   "   " (P. Park "...p. 75
Iron Steamboat Co.'s Time Table..p. 77
Long Island Railroad, Flatbush Av. Time Table...............................p. 79
    "   " Whitehall St. " "................p. 81
    "   " Greenpoint " "................p. 83
    "   " L. I. City " "................p. 85
Horse Car Railroad Time Table...p. 87

Kranich & Bach's Grand, Square and Upright **Pianos,**
On Monthly Installments, A. G. SLADE, Brooklyn Agent, 593 Fulton St.

ILLUSTRATIONS.

Norton's Old Point Comfort House .... p. 7
New York and Brooklyn Bridge .... p. 9
Prospect Park & Coney Island Railroad Map .... p. 11
Depot at West Brighton .... p. 13
Cable's Hotel .... p. 15
Camera Obscura .... p. 17
Observatory .... p. 19
Brighton Pier and Navigation Co .... p. 21
Mrs. Vanderveer's Bathing Pavilion .... p. 23
Bay Ridge Landing, Sea Beach Railroad .... p. 25
Sea Beach Palace Hotel .... p. 27
Ocean Pavilion Hotel .... p. 29
Old Iron Pier .... p. 31
Theatre formerly at West Brighton .... p. 33
Starin's Glen Island .... p. 35
Paul Bauer's West Brighton Hotel .... p. 37
The Argyle .... p. 39
Manhattan Beach Hotel .... pp. 41, 57
Seaside Aquarium .... p. 43
Seaside Home for Children .... p. 45
Brooklyn, Flatbush & Coney Island Railroad Map .... p. 47
Brighton Hotel .... p. 49
Brighton Beach Bathing Pavilion .... p. 51
Bust of G. B. Bunnell .... p. 54
Manhattan Beach Railroad Map .... p. 56
Oriental Hotel .... p. 59
Iron Steamboat .... p. 62

REPRESENTATIVE BUSINESS HOUSES.

Duryea, the Photographer..p. 66
Wilsonia Magnetic Garments..p. 68
Sam'l H. Post, Music dealer..p. 70
Carr & Murray, Carpets, etc..p. 72
H. S. Stewart, Real Estate, etc..p. 74
Henry Affel, Grocer, Teas, etc..p. 74
Weser Brothers, Pianos...p. 76
H. Thimig, bottling, etc...p. 78
Fowler & Wells, Phrenology..p. 80
J. H. Breslin, hotels...p. 82
Brighton Pharmacy..p. 84
Vanderveer's Hotel and Bathing Pavilion............................p. 86
Starin's Glen Island..p. 87
Brighton Racing Association..p. 88
Nelson & Holden, Coal, right top margin of Time Tables.
A. G. Slade, Pianos, right top margin.

A Ramble on the Beach.

By a Pleasure Party.

Coney (or Rabbit) Island was in reality discovered but a few years ago. Prior, it was known only as a sandy waste and windswept region, where the Atlantic surges beat with unrestrained violence; inhabited only by rabbits, "clammers," "roughs" and numerous three-card monte-men, who bore the name of "Coney catchers."

Twenty-five years ago few people dreamed that Coney Island would to-day be *the* watering place of the world; and doubtless we have but a faint conception of its coming greatness and grandeur.

More than three-quarters of this Island was then a barren waste of land, of which even the ownership was doubted, uninhabited save by a few "clammers" and "Coney catchers," who lived back in the swamps of the creek separating it from the main land of Long Island.

Occasionally some target excursion from New York City would charter a dilapidated steamer and sail to the Point for a day's pleasure. A few scattered restaurants, bath-houses and beer saloons were the only places of shelter to be found.

Well does the writer remember, twenty years ago, of paying a visit to Coney Island accompanied by his little boy. We sailed down the bay in an antiquated steamer, mid scenes of confusion and hilarity. At the landing there was a barn-like bar-room, more conspicuous than the dingy dining-room with two barrels at either end supporting boards used as a lunch or dining counter. Chops, chowder, steaks, etc., of a very inferior quality, were purveyed at the prices of fashionable restaurants in the metropolis.

Three-card monte-men and swindlers occupied tables along the beach, which either for bathing purposes or promenade could not be surpassed. It is no exaggeration to say that respectable citizens, and especially ladies, could not visit this Island then without danger of robbery or violence.

Strolling along the beach where one of these swindlers seemed plying his trade with considerable success, we stopped a moment, when a "capper" exclaimed, "I can beat that game!" and turning to us said: "Be kind enough to hold my umbrella, please; me and you can win some money."

Looking with the most profound contempt and disgust at the speaker, the writer said: "Look at me well; do I look like a person you can 'rope into a skin game?'" Humiliated and keenly cut, to think our appearance did not command more respect, we avoided the Island for some years afterward.

Gradually capitalists became awakened to the fact that this spot, as a summer resort and fashionable watering-place, was destined at no distant future to lead the world. Better facilities for reaching this noble breathing-spot, which is providentially so near the Empire City of the Western Continent, now begun to spring into existence. Companies were formed, railroads and iron steamboats built; hotels, restaurants, bathing pavilions, etc., rapidly grew with increased accommodations, until to-day fully 300,000 visitors can be conveyed to and from the beach daily, and find ample entertainment there.

Follow us, reader, in our "Ramble on the Beach," and we will convince you that our assertions are true, and that to-day Coney Island leads the world in point of attractions, bathing, buildings and grandeur.

During one of the extremely hot days of June, "Joe," our friend from boyhood, "Tad," our poetic genius, and "Shaky," our German friend, in company with the writer, left the metropolis for a visit to Coney Island.

We crossed the span known as the "New York and Brooklyn Bridge," without doubt the greatest engineering feat of the century, and eighth wonder of the world, uniting, by the longest span ever made, two of the greatest cities on the continent, of which, in a cablegram, "Consul Prixotti" of Lyons said, "The seven

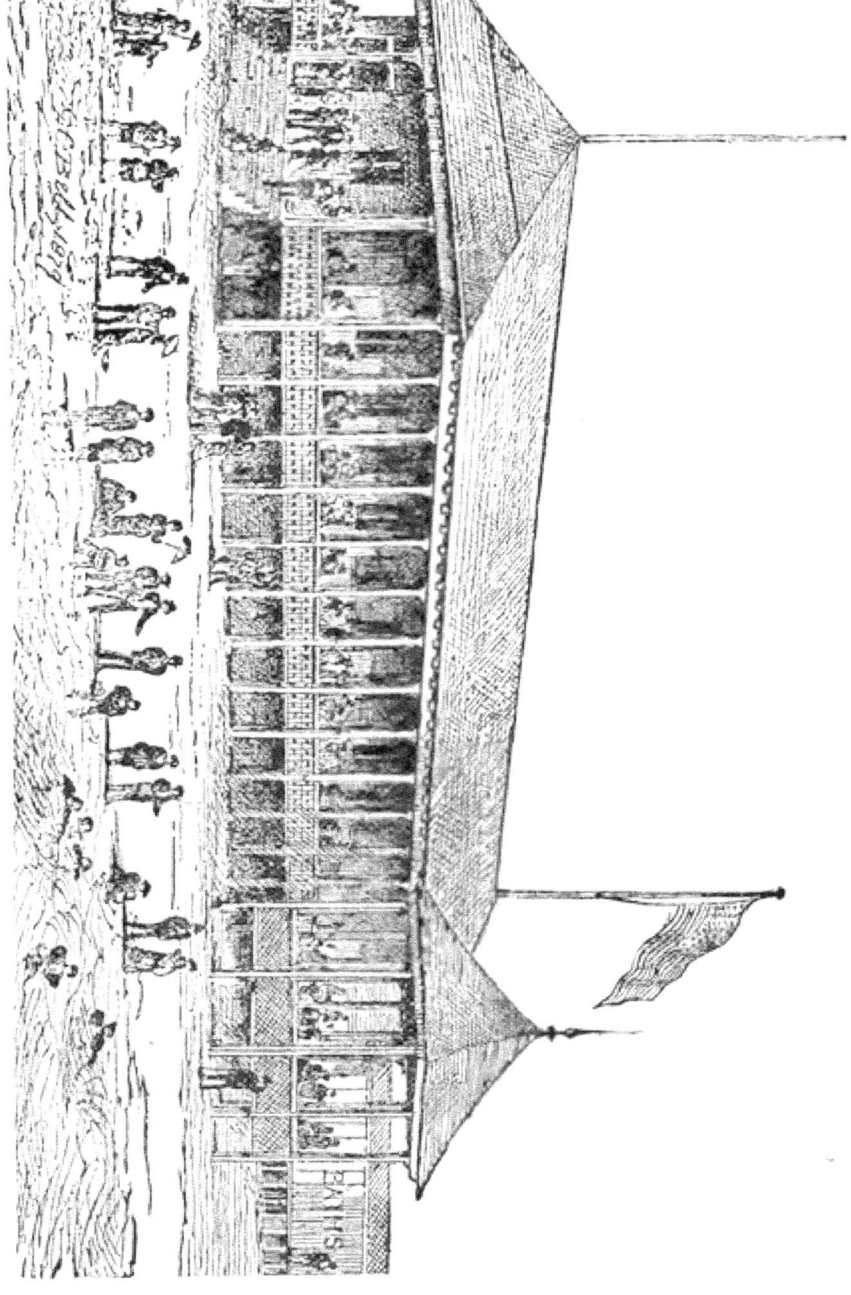

Norton's Old Point Comfort House, West End, Coney Island Point.

wonders dwarf before this one." It was not the work of any one man or of any one age, but the result of many men and many ages.

We quote from an old newspaper published in Brooklyn in 1800, which says:

"It has been suggested that a bridge should be constructed from this village across the river to New York. This idea has been treated as chimerical, from the magnitude of the design; but whosoever takes it into their serious consideration will find more weight in the practicability of the scheme than at first view is imagined. This would be the means of raising the value of the lands on the east side of the river. It has been observed that every objection to the building of this bridge could be refuted, and that it only wanted a combination of opinion to favor the attempt. A plan has already been laid down on paper, and a gentleman of acknowledged abilities and good sense has observed that he would engage to erect it *in two years' time*."

We republish from the "Brooklyn Daily Eagle" the following beautiful poem, which embodies the sentiments of millions of our citizens:

The Brooklyn Bridge.

I stood on the Bridge at sunset,
    While the guns were booming the hour,
And the chimes floated out o'er the water
    From Trinity's grand old tower.

As I gazed on the iron structure
    My thoughts flew on in a dream
Of the masterful mind that had planned it
    To hang o'er the mighty stream.

Of the soul that our Master had taken
    From its home of dissolving clay,
And given a place in His Heaven,
    Whence it views this opening day.

How sadly, O, how sadly,
    Do these mem'ries, rushing aside,
Give room to thoughts of another
    Who's floating still on the tide.

New York and Brooklyn Bridge.

Not in the throng will you find him,
 Not at the festive board,
Not at the head of the workers
 Who toiled so long at his word.

Out through the open window,
 With an eager, glistening eye,
He studies the scene of his labor,
 And the throngs that are hurrying by.

He hears the shrieks of the whistle,
 And the cannon's thundering boom,
And the strains of martial music
 Make an echo in his room.

A smile steals o'er those features,
 So thin, so weary and wan,
But naught can remove from his forehead
 The mark of the deadly caisson.

Ere long he may pass to that future
 So distant, far, and so dim—
He may cross the bridge that the Master
 Has opened to you and to him.

He may meet the one who is waiting
 Just over the dark blue sea,
And together they'll watch o'er the cities
 They have joined so fraternally.—*Bill Arp, Jr.*

Leaving the bridge we board a car, and after a pleasant ride through the streets of the "City of Churches," arrive at the depot of the Prospect Park and Coney Island Railroad, popularly know as "Culver's," and entrance to Greenwood, located at Ninth avenue and Twentieth street. Procuring our tickets we enter the long train of cars in waiting, already quite filled with passengers, and soon speed away to our destination. Passing through a rich, fertile and level country dotted with small but prosperous villages, we listen to the poetic strains of "Tad," as we whirl along. Said he :

" Well I remember when an artless boy,
 And life seemed one continued round of joy !
I visited this spot—how lone it seemed !
But of its future greatness never dreamed.
No railroad lines ran from the cities then ;
No women fair, no proud ambitious men ;
And few who now their frequent visits pay
Had e'er beheld the glorious light of day !
And he who made old Coney Island rise,

Kranich & Bach's Grand, Square and Upright **Pianos,**
On Monthly Installments, A. G. SLADE, Brooklyn Agent, 593 Fulton St.

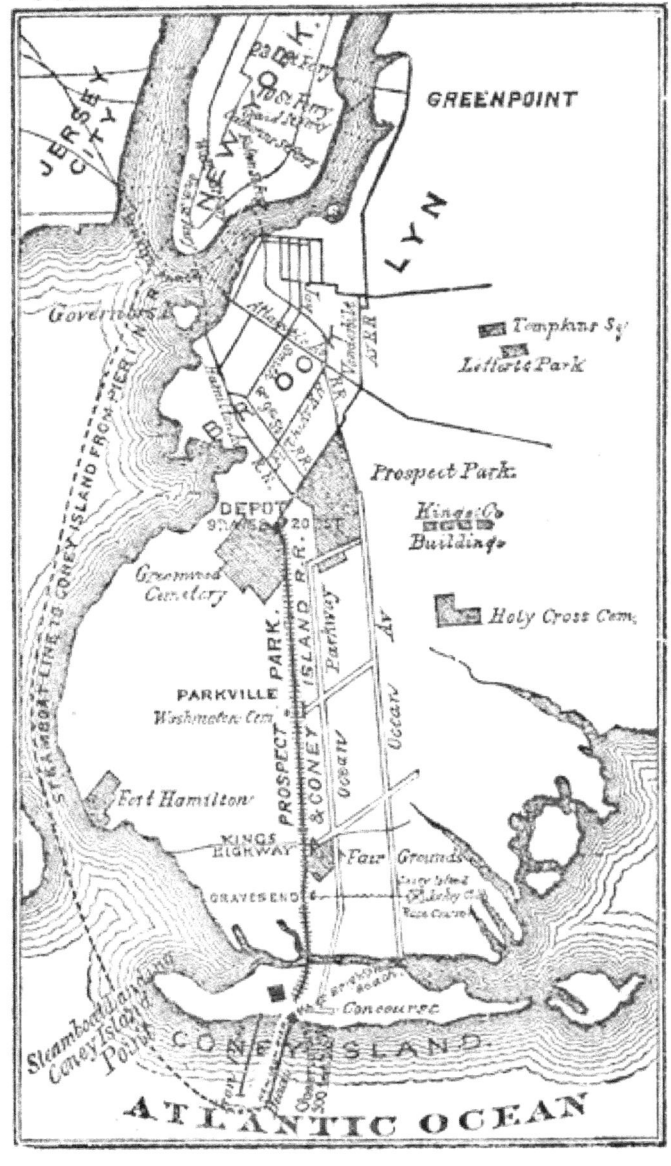

PROSPECT PARK & CONEY ISLAND R.R.

> The tourist's home, the 'People's Paradise,'
> Whose enterprise has raised these magic charms,
> Was but a child in his fond mother's arms.
> But why recount the triumphs, hopes and fears,
> The grand progressive strides of forty years?
> They're but a ripple on the stream of time!
> Whose waters span Eternity sublime!
> And though we count each moment as it flows,
> *Time* had no opening, and can have no close."

So lost were we in "Tad's" improvised poetry that we fell into a reverie until presently "Joe" exclaimed: "Here we are at Coney Island!" Alighting from the train we stood upon a strip of silvery white sand five miles long, separated from Long Island by a narrow creek beyond the portals of the upper bay. The water that breaks in ermine surf along its strand is the pungent and undiluted brine of the Atlantic. The breeze that cools our brow was born far beyond the Gulf stream; and the long rollers that come swelling and breaking at our feet have been sporting with the trade-winds. The waste of waters before us has no nearer boundary than the Eastern hemisphere. The sand glistens in the warm sunshine. Bunting flutters joyously in the sea-breeze from the tops of the buildings, and every pavilion and palace-like structure is swarming with happy people. "This," continued "Joe," "is West Brighton," indicating the picturesque cluster with a wave of his hand. "What great improvements the company have made."

Following the throng through a long covered way, we entered the magnificent new depot. "What a change in comparison with the shed of other seasons," said we, meeting Mr. Culver, the energetic President of this railroad. "Yes," he replied, "all the improvements made since last season cost about $100,000, including the new depot, which is 150 feet long by 50 feet wide, with spacious waiting-room containing an elegant fountain, ladies' parlor finely carpeted and furnished, besides toilet rooms, etc., all illuminated by 20 electric lights in and about the grounds, besides numerous gas jets, which, when lighted, present an admirable appearance to the visitor looking from the outside at the thousand or more stained glass windows.

"The upper portion, reached by this broad staircase from the

Kranich & Bach's Grand, Square and Upright Pianos,
On Monthly Installments, A. G. SLADE, Brooklyn Agent, 593 Fulton St.

Depot P. P. & C. I. R. R., West Brighton, Coney Island.

main waiting-room, is conveniently fitted for offices. We can, with our increased facilities, run in and out of the depot, trains every five minutes in cases of emergency. The marine road running to Coney Island Point leaves this depot, and connects with the Iron steamboats for New York, and all excursion tickets issued by the Iron Steamboat Company at New York will be good to go and return over this route, or either of the Iron Piers, while the return portion of the excursion ticket is good over this road to Brooklyn, including all horse car lines running from its depot to either the Hamilton, South, Wall, Fulton or Catharine Ferries, or the New York and Brooklyn Bridge. All excursion tickets issued by this railroad entitles the holder to admission on the new Iron Pier."

What a grand achievement! The attractions offered the visitor this year are far beyond those of any previous season. The hotel adjoining this depot, formerly known as "Cable's," erected in 1875, the first hotel of any importance on Coney Island, is now conducted by Messrs. Doyle & Stubenbord, in connection with the large lunch pavilion next the ocean frontage.

Standing in the doorway, our eyes rest upon all kinds of mechanical and amusing contrivances. Among them we see the site of the "Bohemian Glass Blowers," "Sea on Land," "Shooting Galleries" and "Rifle Ranges," "Electric Batteries," scales for weighing and testing your height and strength, besides all kinds of accordant and discordant bands and hand-organs blowing and screeching so-called music emanating from various shows.

One young man claims our attention as we near the Iron Pier, shouting to passers-by, "The wonderful 'Camere' is now open, showing you all parts of the island for ten cents." "Vos ish dot?" said Shaky. The Camera Obscura. "De Gamera ob-sura! Veil dot is blain like mud; I like dose tings vot you don'd knows some dings apout, aint it? Dot man makes out der greatest oxcidement; mabe ve don't hat petter see dot alretty?"

We remarked it explained itself better than we, and we would go inside. "Tad" replied to "Shaky" in poetical tones:

"This wondrous Camera minutely paints
Old Coney Island's varied daily drama,
Her joyous children, ladies, "*dudes*" and saints,
In one delightful, living panorama."

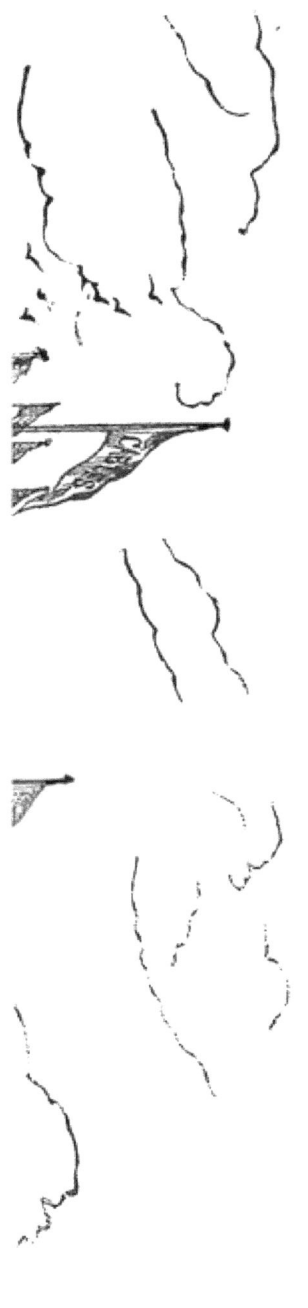

We ascend the steps, and as we enter the room are recognized by Prof. Janton, one of the most fluent and social men on the island, and sole proprietor of this wonderful work of genius. We are inclosed in a darkened room, with lenses placed in such a position in the roof that all surrounding objects within range of the lenses are reflected on a white movable canvas disc. "After a few seconds your eyes will become accustomed to the change of light." "Our first view is the Elevated Railroad; see yonder a train coming in; here the new depot, people coming out; a train has just arrived." "Sthop a leedle," said "Shaky;" "py gracious dot vos der greatest tings: dare coomes Katreen, und de day pack of gesterday she vos told me she nefer goes by dot Goney Island down." We all broke into a hearty laugh simultaneously, which had the effect of quieting "Shaky."

"Step this way," said the Professor. "Here you see the Aquarium, with the 'fat boy' and the 'what is it;' the drive on the Concourse, and Hotel Brighton in the distance; notice, please, the dust from the carriages as they roll along; Mrs. Vanderveer's bathing pavilion; swings in motion; surf breaking in on the beach; step to the left, please. Entrance to the new Iron Pier; see how beautiful the colors show in the flags, and the flowers and vines in the vases; see the wind blowing the flowers back and forth; step to the left, please. Here is West Brighton Hotel; the wonderful cow that gives both milk and lager; Capt. Pierce, the veteran; try your weight before and after bathing." "Oh, what a shame," said an elderly lady to her husband at our elbow; "see" (indicating with her parasol), "there is Mrs. B——, our neighbor, standing there with Mr. J——." "Step this way," said the Professor. "The Sea Beach Palace." "Und dere is Katreen mit anudder fella, so helup my gracious I proke mit a sthick his pack all ofer." "Back again; this ends our exhibition." "This certainly is very clever, the most wonderful and perfect exhibition ever seen," said "Joe," as we emerged from the Camera. "Novelties of art and science from all parts of the old and new world; the most novel and entertaining exhibition on the island; cost you but ten cents; the wonderful Georama."

Looking in the direction from whence comes this solicitation, our eyes rest upon a new building adjoining the largest steam-pro-

Kranich & Bach's Grand, Square and Upright Pianos,

On Monthly Installments, A. G. SLADE, Brooklyn Agent, 593 Fulton St.

Interior of Camera Obscura, during Exhibition, West Brighton, Coney Island.

pelled "Græco-Roman Carrosselle," or merry-go-round, in the country. While lost in admiration of this beautifully painted, Chinese pagoda style of building, with stained glass of all hues in the extension top, Prof. Janton having followed us from the Camera, and tapping our shoulder, said:

"This is the only 'Georama' of the kind in the United States. A capacity to seat thirty people to witness the finest revolving views, true from nature, ever placed before the public. Change of views are made daily from a careful selection of 1,000 choice hand-painted scenes by eminent artists of the old world."

We witness the siege of Paris, and the wonders and beauties of all the principal cities of Europe, Asia, Africa and America, more particularly of Switzerland, Turkey, Italy, Russia, etc., and pronounce it the best and most instructive exhibition for both old and young we have ever seen.

Stepping from the door, we ascend the steps of the Observatory, an iron monster brought at great expense from George's Hill at Philadelphia during the centennial year by Mr. Culver, standing 300 feet above the level of the sea. Said "Tad:"

> "How wonderful to note the mighty power
> Contained in this extensive tower;
> Grand object! rising in the noontide sun,
> The great Centennial Iron Skeleton.
>
> "High o'er the sands this huge but graceful form
> Bids calm defiance to the fiercest storm.
> We mount the car, she gracefully ascends;
> The landscape widens as she upward tends.
>
> "We soon will gain the upper platform high,
> Which seems to hold communion with the sky:
> Gaze, ponder well on land and flood below,
> Nor deem *yourself* the more attractive show.
>
> "Here friends assemble at their sailing hour,
> To view the steamships from the Iron Tower;
> Perchance to watch, with sadness and dismay,
> The ship that bears some loved one far away."

Arriving at the top landing we leave the car and step upon the broad platform, and ascend a flight of winding stairs which lead us to the top. We look in wonder at the panorama below us. Coney Island in all its grandeur lies beneath our feet; our eyes scan the

Kranich & Bach's Grand, Square and Upright Pianos,

On Monthly Installments, A. G. SLADE, Brooklyn Agent, 593 Fulton St.

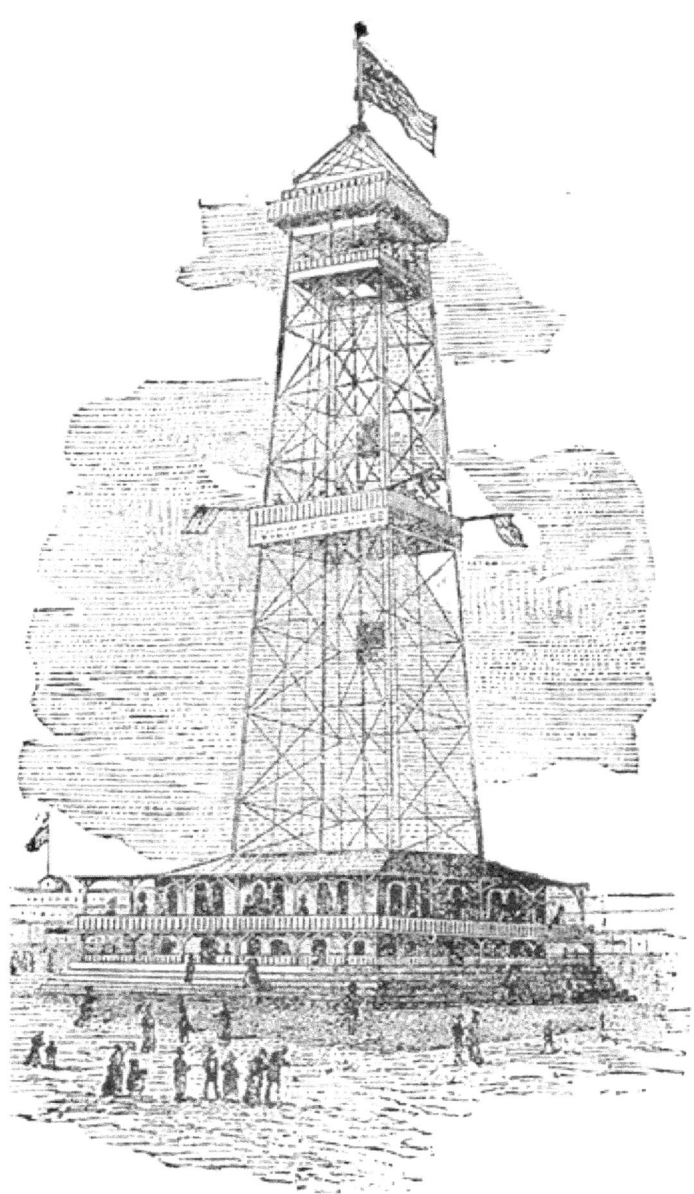

OBSERVATORY AT WEST BRIGHTON, CONEY ISLAND.

zig-zag course of the narrow creek reaching from the "Point" to "Sheepshead Bay," distinctly marking the formation and separation of Coney Island from the mainland. Sounds of all kinds reach our ears from the clangor below; the Concourse, covered with myriads of people and moving vehicles, curves gracefully inside of the surf line; while the palatial hotels appear like miniature buildings in fairy-land. An immense telescope surmounts this lofty tower, with lenses of powerful magnitude and penetrating power, reaching as far as Long Branch, a distance of 25 miles south; Highlands of Neversink, 13 miles; Sandy Hook, 8 miles; Point Comfort, 13 miles; Keyport, 17 miles; Norton's Point, 2 miles west; Fort Wadsworth, 5 miles; Hoboken and Jersey City, 12 miles; High Bridge tower, 20 miles north; Brooklyn suburbs, 8 miles; Jamaica, 14 miles; Hempstead Plains and Garden City, 20 miles; Rockaway beach 8 miles east, and Sandy Hook lightship, 12 miles; besides numerous intermediate points.

Said "Shaky:" "Does vos der piggest dings owid, beobles all der dimes foolishness und humpugs makes ven day look py does leedle sphy-glazzes owid; but ven day py does pig spy-glazzes look, den dot vos no foolishness. I makes me owid some leedle boedry on dot:

    Ven I vas mit dot sphy-glazzes look owid,
    I zee mineseluff dwendy miles aboud.
    Py chimminy cracious! Does dings vos immensus,
    Ven I look by der hole mit dot ofulest lenzes.

    I zee does blaces dot far avay peen,
    Und ships dot mit under gundries vos kin;
    Does stheeples by Brooklyn-town 8 miles avay,
    Und beebles by Prighton mit vouter makes play.

    Free cracious fur noddings, I dole you does dings,
    Id costen den cents, ven dot glazzes you prings,
    Und zee dot gundree all rount apout.
    Und der Proffessor vot makes you does dings all owid."

We were astonished and withal much pleased at "Shaky's" poetical effusion. Certainly he had caught the inspiration from "Tad," and his imaginative powers were striving to grasp that intuition which marks the born poet.

As we descend in the car the landscape gradually fades from

Brighton Pier and Navigation Co., West Brighton, Coney Island.

our view, and objects which before seemed miniature now assume their proper proportions. We alight, and after a moment's walk enter the BRIGHTON PIER, which is, without exception, the finest structure of its kind in the United States, if not in the world.

Reaching out a distance of 1,500 feet in the ocean, and having a width of 150 feet at each end, of novel and artistic design, it stands as a worthy monument to the fame of the designer. At the extreme ocean end there is a pavilion two stories high, the upper story having a seating capacity of 2,500, surmounted by a magnificent dome illuminated at night by numerous electric lights. This portion of the Pier is now utilized as a theatre, known as the "Brighton Theatre," under the management of Mr. Donaldson, of the London Theatre, New York city, enterprising and well qualified to fill the position. Performances of a light but pleasing character—such as first-class operatic, theatrical and variety entertainments—are given every afternoon and evening during the season. A fine large stage with artistic scenic effect, capable of producing most any drama successfully, occupies a conspicuous position. Front rows of seats are especially reserved for ladies and children without escorts, and every essential provision is made for the comfort of visitors.

Certainly a most novel and original idea—a theatre on the rolling billows of the great Atlantic, where you may enjoy an evening's entertainment without the unpleasant feeling of sea-sickness, and at the same time be fanned by the cool breeze of the ocean, while seated above the waves. A more delightful spot during the sultry days of summer is not to be found than on this Pier.

We next visit Mrs. Vanderveer's Bathing Pavilion, situated at right angles as we emerge from the Brighton Pier, with a broad beach, smooth as glass, leading into the dancing, foaming waters. One of the most commodious structures of its kind on the Atlantic coast is here found, with an ocean frontage of nearly two hundred feet in length by one hundred feet wide, having a capacity for accommodating one thousand bathers at the same time.

The laundry is perfection in itself. A few years since, at Coney Island, if a visitor desired to bathe, he was provided with a suit that was still wet with previous use, with towels in a clammy state of moisture, and with a toilet room of unplaned boards.

Kranich & Bach's Grand, Square and Upright **Pianos,**
On Monthly Installments, A. G. SLADE, Brooklyn Agent, 593 Fulton St.

Mrs. Vanderveer's Bathing Pavilion, West Brighton, Coney Island.

Ladies were compelled to use rooms next to those of offensive men, whose conversation could be distinctly heard. Instead, we here found accommodations on the second floor for the sexes separated, and each bathing suit thoroughly cleansed and dried by steam. Five hundred suits can be washed and dried in twenty minutes. A large Marvin safe is provided with five hundred separate apartments for the deposit of valuables during bath. Twenty large electric lights illuminate this magnificent structure and grounds, enabling bathing to be continued after dark, and lifeguards in boats patrol the water to prevent accidents. An elegant and costly furnished parlor is provided for ladies on the first floor, while in the middle tower are several finely fitted rooms with all improvements for gentlemen by the week. A notable feature is the hot and cold salt water baths in the building. Perfect privacy is here had. If the sea water at its natural temperature is too severe, persons who wish it may enjoy in-doors a bath heated to any degree that suits them.

We enter one of the many dressing-rooms, and, after disrobing, don our bathing costumes preparatory to a splash in the cool, inviting waters. As we descend the long covered way and step upon the beach, "Tad," in a humorous and sarcastical frame of mind, chipped as follows:

> "On this loved spot the timid, gay and grave,
> Seek health and pastime in the briny wave;
> There tumble topsy-turvy, 'thick as spatter!'
> Like animalcules in a drop of water,
> The little child just learning how to swim;
> The athlete ponderous, with the brawny limb;
> The spruce Apollo (dude), with his parted hair,
> Beside the swaggering, bloated millionaire,
> For snobs ascend to feelings democratic,
> When they *descend* to healthy sports aquatic.

> "The country rustic and the city swell,
> The Western beauty and the city belle;
> The Jersey farmer, with an honest face,
> The "prancing preacher," with the *means* of grace;
> The ancient "bay-bag"—comical to see—
> Contrasted with a queen de Medici!
> Long-faced dead-beats, tho' never "*called*" to preach—
> Are *ranked* as BEECHERS when they're "on the beach."

Kranich & Bach's Grand, Square and Upright Pianos,
On Monthly Installments, A. G. SLADE, Brooklyn Agent, 593 Fulton St.

BAY RIDGE LANDING, SEA BEACH R. R.

We roll in the surf for awhile with numerous others, enjoying the air and sea with more beneficial results than many doses of the most potent elixir of life ever concocted. Emerging from the water much exhilarated, we enter our bathing-room and dress.

With a keen appetite whetted by the sea air, and fully determined to investigate the mysteries of the chowder, etc., as served at Coney Island, we follow a crowd of promenaders who surged along the broad Concourse until we arrived at the Sea Beach Palace Hotel. Here was animation, variety and brilliancy. This beautiful, spacious building, formerly occupied by the United States Government, was brought at great expense from the Centennial Exposition at Philadelphia. Among a group of gentlemen we espied our friend, Mr. W. O. McDowell, Vice-President and General Manager of the Sea Beach Railroad, with his genial smile; and as we approached and engaged him in conversation, we learned that the Railroad Company had been thoroughly reorganized and bought in for the first mortgage bonds by a syndicate of wealthy gentlemen. The same syndicate, owning their own steamboats, are the only company delivering passengers direct at Coney Island from New York without having to pay money to other companies or steamboats; being in position, therefore, to give the quickest time and at less expense of any route to the Island, besides avoiding all unpleasant smells and sea-fogs.

This syndicate of gentlemen having been blessed with the genius of prophetic intuition which makes the successful engineers, inventors and capitalists, with a capacity to foresee that which everybody lightly says, when the object has been attained, "might have been foreseen by an infant."

Says our keen perceptive friend, "The exposition which we inaugurate here this season is intended to pave the way for the World's Fair at Coney Island in connection with which New York is soon to outdo that which Philadelphia accomplished with her Centennial Exposition in 1876." "This," said he, "has been delayed up to the present time for the want of a place where all the railroads entering New York City could compete with equal opportunities. Coney Island now furnishes this place with her railroads and steamboats equal to conveying any number of people, and her hotels of New York City and Rockaway with ample

Kranich & Bach's Grand, Square and Upright Pianos,

On Monthly Installments, A. G. SLADE, Brooklyn Agent, 593 Fulton St.

SEA BEACH PALACE HOTEL, WEST BRIGHTON, CONEY ISLAND.

capacity to furnish all needed entertainments. An additional advantage is offered, in, that all buildings erected in connection with the exposition would be continually available for a permanent exhibition at this famous resort, and would be most certainly sustained by her average 80,000 visitors now daily and continually increasing."

We chimed in a hearty response to this novel and original idea, and thought how obvious was it that in the vapor which James Watt saw issuing from his mother's tea-kettle reposed the power which now propels mighty steamers across the ocean and draws trains of palace cars across a continent; or that a cord of guttapercha, hemp and wire could convey messages from the old to the new world. Yet the theories of James Watt were laughed at ; the projectors of the Atlantic cable sought for supporters to their enterprise in vain. A Columbus or a Fulton crystallizes an idea, which has found lodgement in the brains of thousands who could never formulate it, and when it is expressed these thousands exclaim : " How true—how often we have felt it."

Hurrying along the spacious piazza, looking for the best accommodations to offer his guests, until our party was reached, when, with a " How are you ; how d'do ; glad to see you " kind of manner, we recognize our old friend, E. D. Myers, Brooklyn's favorite caterer, and now manager of the hotel and restaurant at this point. The service was of the highest order, and the dinner, with its various courses, ample to satisfy any *connoisseur*, and infinitely superior to that of any other watering-place in point of quality, quantity and price, being served to guests by attentive lady waiters, with bill of fare at popular New York prices, such as found at Smith & McNell's popular hotel in the metropolis (ignoring Coney Island prices). Said our host, " We will serve in centre of main diningroom a shore or full dinner for 75 cts., and at the "bargain counter" all cold cuts with perquisites at 25 cts. each." Ten thousand guests can here find accommodation over night, and a capacity for seating and feeding fifteen thousand persons at the same time. Mr. C. F. Armstrong, well and favorably known on Coney Island, has the bar privilege, where he dispenses the choicest wines and liquors. Finally, after lighting a cigar, no Eastern potentate can appreciate the meaning of superlative luxury better than we at this moment.

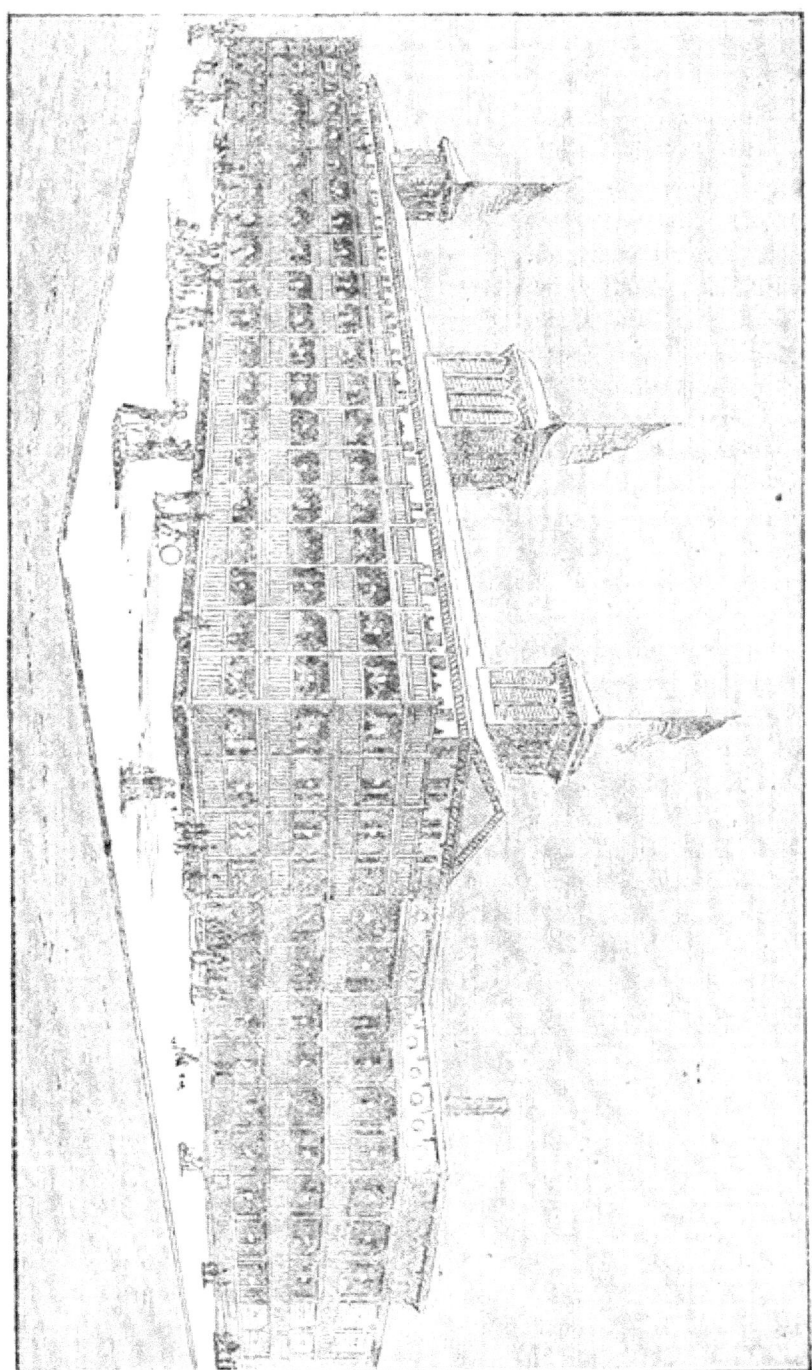

Chas. Feltman's Ocean Pavilion, West Brighton, Coney Island.

Directly opposite, we enter the Ocean Pavilion, the largest and most spacious building on Coney Island, having 138,000 square feet of flooring. This magnificent structure, owned and managed by Mr. Charles Feltman, the pioneer of the island—a gentleman of great executive capacity, who unites a suavity of manner and an amiability of demeanor, very attractive qualities which are too often lacking in those whose business it is to cater to the wants of the public—is the chief point of attraction at this portion of the beach to "connoisseurs" of the Terpsichorean art.

At every point we see great improvements having been made since last season. We ascend to the large ball-room, illuminated by 11 electric lights and 400 gas jets, being 223 feet in length by 45 feet wide, and capable of accommodating 3,000 dancers at one time. The oil paintings on the panels of this room are magnificent, being finer than those of any like room on this continent; the ocean end panels representing, in beautiful characters, Spring, Summer, Autumn and Winter, while those on the side are finely executed landscape scenes, etc., by a masterly hand. The soul-enchanting music from a band of 20 performers falls upon our ears in sweet cadences, inviting us to join the dancers, who are now whirling in the giddy waltz. As we view the merry tripping feet from a window of the broad piazza, capable of seating comfortably 5,000 guests, we catch a glimpse of "Shaky," whom we had not before missed, enjoying this fascinating accomplishment with quite a fine-looking blonde; too much engaged to hear our shout "Shaky!" "Shaky!" The dance goes on and so do we.

Strolling along the crowded piazza, "Tad" gives expression to his feelings, saying:

> "Here's lots of fun" enjoyed by man.
>   Dancing with pleasant folks, and queer;
> The *Ocean Pavilion* kept by *Feltman*,
>   Claims, mirth was *made* the heart to cheer.
>
> Such spacious room cannot be found,
>   Look where you will, in every part
> Of Coney Island's pleasure ground,
>   This beats 'em all for dance and art."

Said "Joe," "Here comes Mr. Feltman, the proprietor, one of the most jolly, energetic, frank and open-hearted men on the beach; I will introduce you."

Kranich & Bach's Grand, Square and Upright Pianos,

On Monthly Installments, A. G. SLADE, Brooklyn Agent, 593 Fulton St.

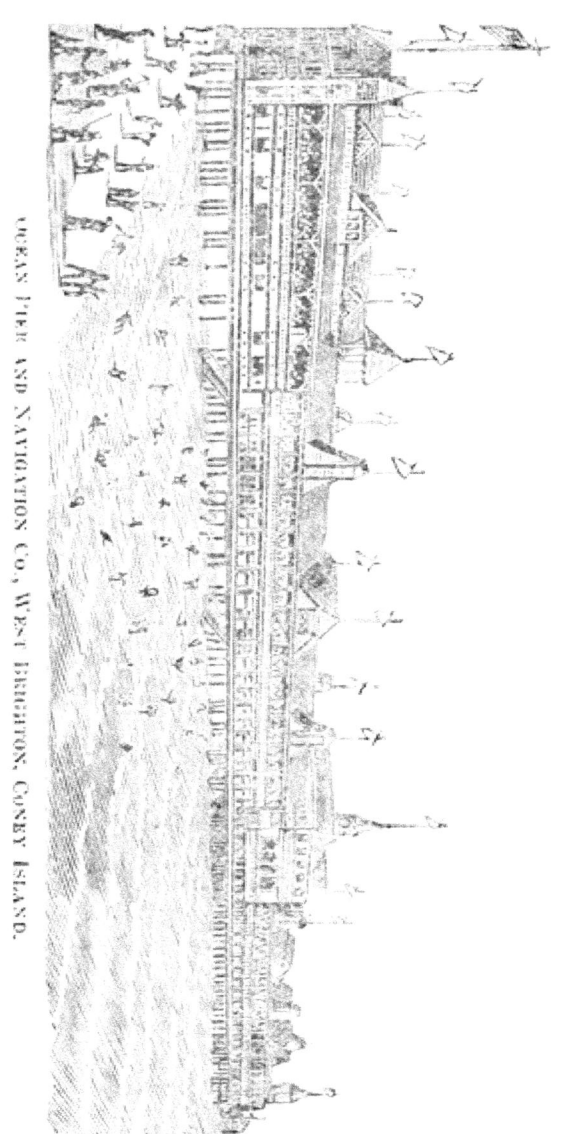

OCEAN PIER AND NAVIGATION CO., WEST BRIGHTON, CONEY ISLAND.

Being welcomed very hearty by a warm grasp of the hand, after the formality of an introduction, Mr. Feltman, familiarly known as "Charley," said: "About nine years ago, when I first contemplated coming here, friends said I was 'crazy' to think of investing money in a white sand bank, and the only person that gave me any encouragement was 'Mr. Culver.' I *knew money* could be made here; I obtained an eleven years' lease of this property, including the land occupied by the Sea Beach Hotel, at a yearly rental of $25. The property was in the market, but no one would have it. The first season I opened I engaged ' Wannemacher's 71st Regt. Band,' which was the first that ever played on the Island under like circumstances.

"The following season I was the first to introduce vocal music here; since then instrumental and vocal music are among the greatest attractions on this Island. I took all risks, and feel that I have had my full share of the patronage."

Accommodations for 20,000 people at the same time, with ample room for seating 5,000 comfortably, are here offered. Many of the old patrons of this establishment would hardly recognize the place now, so extensive have been the improvements since last season. $20,000 have been expended, and probably $10,000 more will be required to complete it. 118 rooms for the accommodation of boarders have recently been fitted up in the upper portion of this immense pavilion; each one large and airy, carpeted with velvet and Brussels, containing marble wash-basins and gas. The Summer Garden, recently enlarged, is now 155 feet long by 57 feet wide, containing some three hundred evergreen trees closely planted in large boxes along the sides.

Mr. Fred. Roberts, the well-known and popular vocal comedian, is director of amusements; nothing but the finest artists in the profession (variety) have been engaged, and those acquainted with the talents of "Fred." know that he is well qualified to fill any position he may accept.

Since the improvements made, better facilities are offered for the purpose of festivals for large societies, lodges and clubs. Already arrangements have been made with the following: July 10, the "Nerddeutschen Brueder" (North German Brothers), with 2,500 admission tickets; July 11, the "Lamstedter Society," with

Kranich & Bach's Grand, Square and Upright Pianos,

On Monthly Installments, A. G. SLADE, Brooklyn Agent, 593 Fulton St.

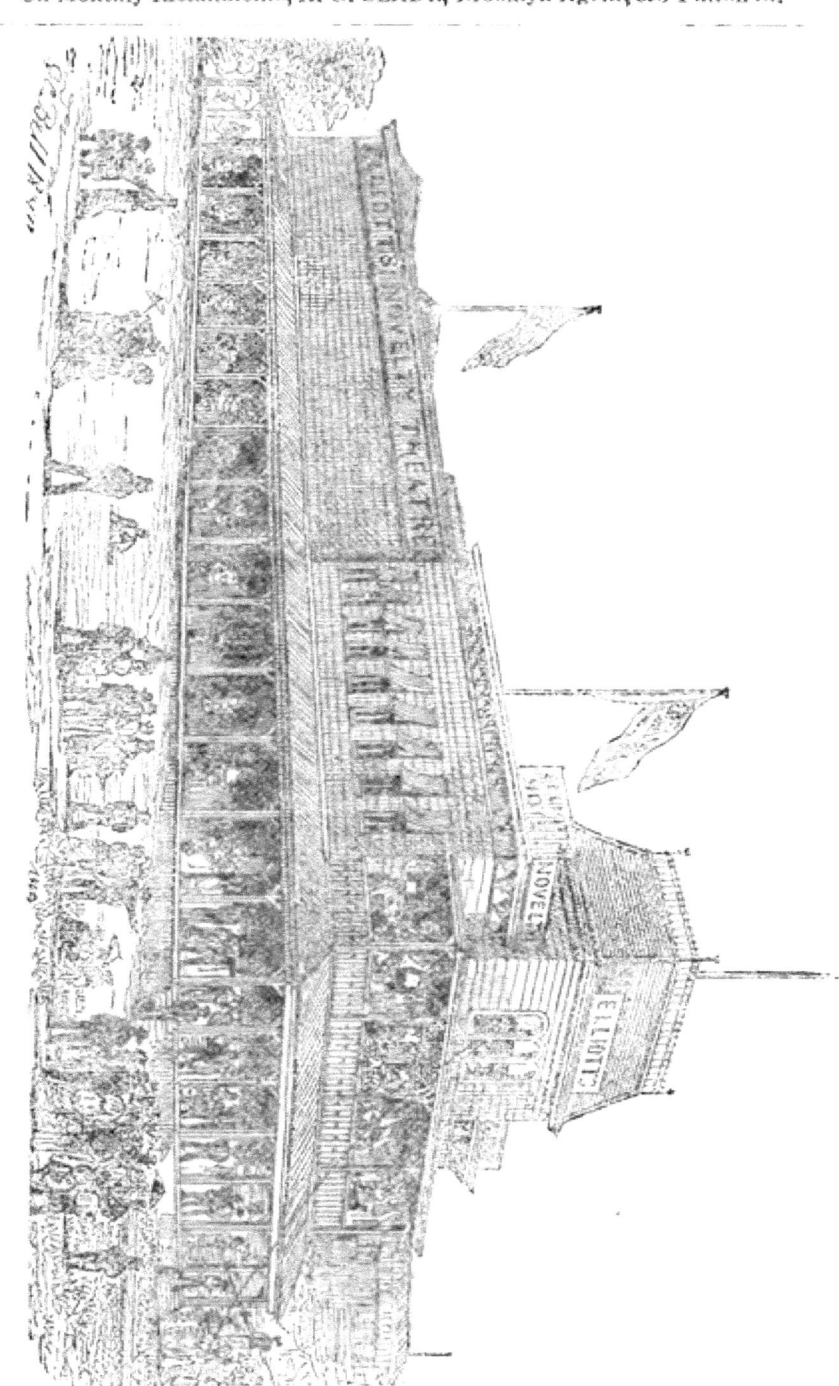

Theatre Formerly at West Brighton, Coney Island.

2,500 admission tickets; July 12, the "Brooklyn Young Butcher Guards," with 3,000 admission tickets; July 16, the "Harmonia Maennerchor," with 4,000 admission tickets; July 17, "Weber's Dancing Academy," with 3,000 admission tickets; July 19, the "Bremervoerder Society," with 3,000 admission tickets; July 23, the United "Lodges of Knights" and "Ladies of Honor," with 5,000 admission tickets; July 25, the "Washington Lodge," with 2,500 admission tickets; July 26, the United Lodges of the "German Order of Haragari," with 8,000 admission tickets; July 30, the "Scandinavian Singing Society," with 2,500 admission tickets; Aug. 7, the "Fritz Reuter Lodge," with 2,000 admission tickets; August 15, the "Ringgold Mutual Association," with 3,000 admission tickets; August 16, the Grand Lodge of the "A. O. of G. F.," under the auspices of 19 lodges, with 8,000 admission tickets; August 23, "South Brooklyn Turners and Thalia Singing Society," with 3,500 admission tickets; August 30, the "Brooklyn Schuetzen Corps," with 3,500 admission tickets, besides other smaller festivals held every night during the season.

Arrangements are made with Mr. Feltman by most of the societies whereby he furnishes transportation; several, however, from New York, come by way of Bay Ridge, by boat, to the depot of the Sea Beach R. R. This certainly is a very pleasant sail along the slopes of the shore of Long Island, whose banks are lined with villages of greater or less attraction as far as the eye can reach, until lost in the Narrows.

Strains of music, soft and gentle, fell upon our ears as we neared the Concourse. Following the sound, we were led to the "West Brighton Hotel," into the presence of the only female band on Coney Island, known as the "Vienna Female Orchestra," comprising thirty performers, led by Mrs. Marie Roller, all elegantly attired.

Where language, as an expressive power, ceases, music begins; and to say we were lost in rapture and wonderment, would be but mockery, as we listened to these soul-inspiring strains, as one after another of the various changes were rendered in perfect time and accord, with admirable taste. Now a soft, bird-like trill, followed by that of other warblers, gradually increasing in volume until the whole air seemed filled with feathery songsters;

Kranich & Bach's Grand, Square and Upright Pianos,

On Monthly Installments, A. G. SLADE, Brooklyn Agent, 593 Fulton St.

"Starin's" Glen Island, Long Island Sound.

then floating away gently in smooth, silvery tones, now in a light, playful and sportive manner, with a division of rapid flight, feeling and sentiment, producing a tremulous kind of emotion, increasing with briskness and animation; then diminishing by degrees, steadily, with pathos, gradually dying and floating away.

Oh, tranquil moment, how peaceful, how divine! In music the mind is at rest, the heart's turmoil becomes quiet, and the spirit basks in the peaceful delights of sweet repose. Such were the thoughts swelling our minds when the spell was broken by an exclamation of:

"Fine music, gentlemen!"

Gladly we recognize the voice of Mr. Paul Bauer, sole proprietor of this greatly enlarged, airy and comfortable palace-like structure, 242 feet long by 128 feet wide, capable of seating 6,000 people comfortably at the same time. To Mr. Bauer, who is the manager and superintendent of all this immense business, is due the honor of having the largest and most tastefully decorated and illuminated room under one roof of any place on Coney Island. Hotel accommodations with him are secondary, still he has a large number of rooms elegantly fitted up to accommodate 200 guests, with private dining rooms, and four tower rooms, finely furnished, for the especial use of coaching parties.

The kitchen has all the requirements for catering to 8,000 guests daily, and in several instances 10,000 visitors have been dined with complete satisfaction to themselves.

A new wine and store room has recently been added with a capacity for 20,000 bottles at the same time, besides all kinds of canned goods: this is under the control of Mr. J. L. Steinhardt, assistant manager to Mr. Bauer, an affable and pleasant gentleman, qualified in all respects to fill this responsible and trustworthy position. A very large patent refrigerator, costing $1,800, has recently been erected. The centre apartment has three perpendicular, galvanized iron tubes about one foot in diameter by ten feet long, filled with cracked ice and salt from the store room. An opening behind the bar reveals elegantly arranged tiers of shelving for bottles; this apartment can be reduced to a temperature of 10 degrees, and by opening the door can be brought up to 40 degrees

Paul Bauer's West Brighton Hotel, West Brighton, Coney Island.

in a few moments—certainly the most economical and best arranged refrigerator on the Atlantic coast.

The open space on the ocean frontage of the piazza formerly given to excursionists who come provided with their own luncheons, has undergone marked changes since last season. The space has been devoted to serving excellent 50-cent dinners.

This grand structure is illuminated by 46 electric lights and 1,000 gas jets with various colored glass globes.

Although the hour was growing late, still crowds of pleasure seekers were perambulating the beach, and the luminous moon shone down tranquil and silent upon the scene, while the rythmic beat of the waves along the shore played and twinkled with myriad diamond-points reflected in the moonlight.

We found an inviting broad piazza at Mrs. Vanderveer's hotel, where we could sit secluded and still enjoy the beautiful scene and a good cigar. Strains of vocal music floated upon our ears from the parlor from some lady-singer, whose voice was exquisitely soft and sweet ; as she trilled out the notes we fell into a pleasant reverie, and, having finished our cigars, we retired to our respective rooms and were lulled to sleep by the ceaseless splash of waves upon the beach.

After a comfortable rest we arose ; the morning hours were soft and cool, and a wondrously beautiful light fell on the ocean. As we looked from our window, the distant Jersey highlands became a purple, tinged with gold, and the waves seemed crisp, glassy, and fringed with foam, and as they leaped into peaks the light flashes through them, and shows how green they are. We descend to the dining-room. The table is spread with snowy linen, and sparkles with crystal ware ; the waiters civil and intelligent. We order breakfast ; sirloin steak, toast and fried potatoes, with a cup of fragrant Mocha, which appeases our appetites.

After breakfast we light a cigar, and, seated on the upper piazza, dream of fairy-land, perfectly resigned to bliss, at least as near as mortal man can attain it.

Being aroused by the appproach of "Shaky" entering our presence, he said (but we let him tell his own story) :

"Vell, I don'd vos no fool ; gesterday night ven I go by mineseluf avay, I zee me Katreen mid dot lofer feller come by dot eading

Kranich & Bach's Grand, Square and Upright Pianos,

On Monthly Installments, A. G. SLADE, Brooklyn Agent, 593 Fulton St.

"The Argyle," New Hotel at Babylon, L. I.

houses owid. Dot drives avay mine batience airetty, und I dinks me I knock dot feller's nose by der back of hees het arount; und Katreen coomes by me up und sayt, 'Shaky, I vos glat vat I zeen you pen here.' Vell, I dink der dime vos coomes ven I makes mine foot down right avay gwick, un dole to Katreen vot pizness vos. I sayt, dot vos a shame ven you mit dot lofer Irishman Goney Island valk arount. I vos mat, und shump minesleuf up und down; shoost den dot Irishman coomes by me up und sayt:"

"Ma-ark moi wurruds Tutchy, if yeez's bother ony moore wud me gal, I'll lick yeez widin an inch av yer durthy scaurkrooting, lager-guzzling, haythen life av yeez."

"I sayt dot vos all right, und bressed hess hant in zilence, un spheak me not annder vort: but I vos looking abowit me for dot boleecerman, ven dot Irishman sayt:"

"D'ye moind, niver a worrud from yeez, molist her no moore, or by the soul av me, I'll bate yeez durthy mug wid me chew fists. None av yer dutch blab, yeez gaarlick-sthuffin, limburger atin sphalpeen, yeez."

"I dink dot Irishman vos got mat booty gwick, un der long sthory vos better made shortness of, so I spheak minesluf noddings, un valk der rote down."

"Certainly, you acted the most sensible part," said Joe. "Always avoid that which may lead to trouble. The better part of valor is to run away instead of fight. And that reminds me of a little rhyme I learned when a mere schoolboy. I think it is,

'He who lives to run away,
May live to fight another day.'"

"Yez, dot ish drue," said "Shaky." "I like dot booty goot. Vell, I go by der dancing houses down, un sthandt me by der hostes up, un der man he sayt to me,"

"Go by der sthaircases up un zee der dance."

"I vos by dose sthairs valken up, ven an under man sayt,"

"Dicked!"

"Vos ish dot?"

"Dicked! Dot vos costen haluf toller ven you by der dance

Kranich & Bach's Grand, Square and Upright Pianos,
On Monthly Installments, A. G. SLADE, Brooklyn Agent, 593 Fulton St.

Manhattan Beach Hotel, Coney Island.—(During Balloon Ascension.)

coome up. Go by der stairs down un got von dicked by dot man vot in der vinder look owid."

"I dink does vos booty small berdaders, ven dot costen haluf toller. Vell, I pay me dot und go by der door insite, un sit me by der dable down. Py chiminy! von vimens coomes un set mit me. I like dot booty much, un laff me so much I got von stomich ake by mine het. Ven I by der school hauses go, dot vos bunishment ven a poy vos set a girl 'longside of, un I dink I now bunish mine-seluf alretty. I make me zum leedle boedry on dot."

> "I dold to dot vaiterman zwie lager beer,
> Un ven I sayt dot, I hear me so glear,
> Dot vimen she holler't un bointed me owid,
> Py cracious! I zee me dot Irishman aboud.
>
> "So hellup me chiminy! I shump me up guick,
> Katreens lofer feller coomes mit me a stick,
> I vos fallen me owid, der pack vinder sashes,
> Yoost ven I dot gal vas getten der mashes."

Strolling along the beach, we find it crowded with promenaders, and children with shovels and pails digging clams. The sea was beautiful, and away in the distance we see outward bound steamers and white sails near the shore of the Highlands of Neversink, while about us the shore wore the appearance of a French *fete*.

During our stroll we enter the Seaside Aquarium, under the management of Mr. Bradenburgh. Here are all kinds of animals, fish and curiosities. While looking at an immense bear, "Shaky" says:

"Dole me abowt dose; I zee dot sthandt on der bapers pout der pulls un pears by Voll sthreedt, un under vild pestus by der oxchange sthock; vot it meanish by dot? Dot baper sayt dey shnap un shnarl. I dink vot vood dems proker mans do ven does animals vos loosen got."

Said Mr. Bradenburgh, "These animals are not quite as ferocious as those our German friend speaks of; in comparison they are quite docile; but gentlemen, step inside and be seated, the stage performance is about to begin."

While in the auditorium we witness an excellent entertainment under the direction of Prof. F. H. Hoffman, stage manager, and

Kranich & Bach's Grand, Square and Upright Pianos,
On Monthly Installments, A. G. SLADE, Brooklyn Agent, 593 Fulton St.

Seaside Aquarium, West Brighton, Coney Island.

the best aerial suspension performer and conjurer we have ever seen, also the performing birds; Mr. J. C. Leech, Chinese impersonator and imitator of animals; Miss Nellie Collins, songstress, and the Parker brothers in songs and dance; and Frank West, champion roller skater. The juggling on the slack wire by a lady artist was something wonderful; certainly this act alone was well worth the price of admission, besides the immense collection of rare animals from foreign countries, together with various fish from the sounding sea. Said "Tad,"

> "Seaside Aquarium delight affords,
> In each terrestrial and aquatic mystery:
> And daily holds its intellectual hordes,
> Who take an interest in natural history."

The "Seaside Home for Children," located on the Old Plank Road, near the terminus of the horse cars, directly in rear of the Aquarium, and under the auspices of the Brooklyn Aid Society, offers a shelter to thousands of poor sick children during the season.

A few days at this Home saves the lives of many poor weak and suffering children, who have breathed no purer air than such as is usually found in some hot overcrowded tenement house in a thickly portion of the city.

Visitors are invited each day of the week, except Sunday. Taking advantage of this we enter the gate, and are welcomed by Mr. R. D. Douglass, the efficient and untiring Superintendent. We found a very spacious, roomy, airy and comfortable Home in every respect. Numerous little ones were clinging to the hands, legs and coat of Mr. Douglass, while others were running about and playing various games.

"The Home," said Mr. Douglass, "seeks to benefit children with diseases incident to the hot weather, where change of air is more beneficial than medicine; children under five years old have the preference, and mothers are admitted with their children when necessary. Those with contagious diseases are not admitted."

"Somewhat limited in room, still we accommodate all until the Home is filled, regardless of creed or nationality, and all is absolutely free. To prevent disappointment, every application for

Kranich & Bach's Grand, Square and Upright **Pianos,**

On Monthly Installments, A. G. SLADE, Brooklyn Agent, 593 Fulton St.

SEASIDE HOME FOR CHILDREN, WEST BRIGHTON, CONEY ISLAND.

admission must be made at the Brooklyn office, 31 Sands street."

"We are now entering the eighth year of our work; during the past seven years 15,705 children and 5,568 mothers have spent a short time in the Home. Words cannot tell what amount of good has been done, or how many lives have been saved. We depend entirely upon voluntary gifts from those who are in sympathy with our work, for the maintenance of this Home. One hundred dollars cares for more than sixty children for a week, $50 for thirty, and $10 for six."

Reader, we appeal to you in behalf of this noble cause.

How many children will you aid? The smallest contributions are gratefully accepted and promptly acknowledged by the Superintendent.

Bathing suits, muslin and linen pieces, or quilts, are of the greatest service; also women's or children's clothing and baby carriages. The co-operation of physicians, city missionaries, Sunday school and Christian workers generally, of any denomination, are earnestly requested to bring proper cases to the notice of the Superintendent.

Brighton Beach, Coney Island, is reached in a variety of ways, but by none so safely and expeditiously as the Brooklyn, Flatbush and Coney Island Railroad, which runs directly to the Brighton Beach Hotel. The depots of this line are located at the junction of Flatbush and Atlantic avenues, adjoining the armory of the Thirteenth Regiment; Franklin, corner of Atlantic avenue, and at Prospect Park, Willink entrance.

Gordon L. Ford, Esq., President of this road, is exerting every possible effort to accommodate the public and benefit the stockholders. Entering the depot at Flatbush avenue, we provide ourselves with the necessary letters of introduction, i. e., tickets, pass the gatekeeper, and enter one of the excursion cars just in time to hear the conductor's cheery "All aboard."

As we start, we wonder what our company is for the next twenty minutes, that being about the time usually occupied in running to the beach. The car is full of ladies, gentlemen and children, all bent on having a good time, and no place better could they seek it than that for which they have started.

We pass out of the depot into Atlantic avenue—an iron fence

Kranich & Bach's Grand, Square and Upright Pianos,

On Monthly Installments, A. G. SLADE, Brooklyn Agent, 593 Fulton St.

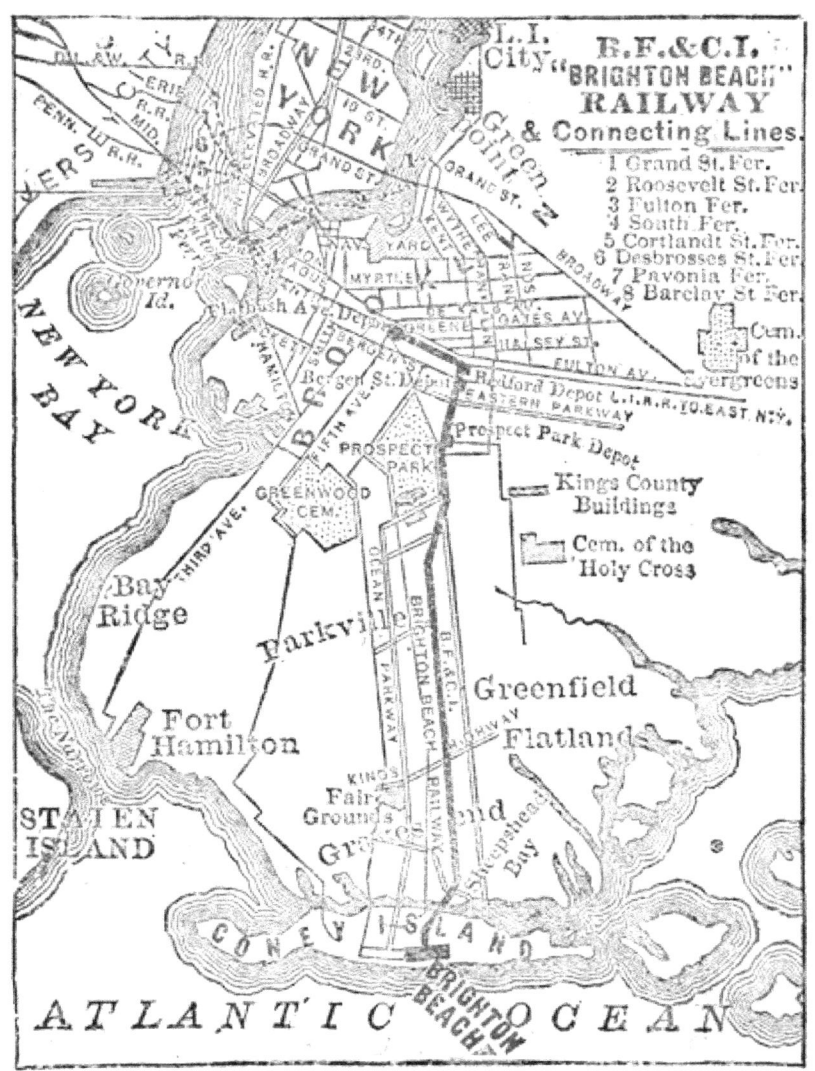

Map of B. F. & C. I. R. R.

inclosing the tracks, and each crossing guarded by gates, with watchmen in attendance to protect pedestrians and vehicles from passing trains. Gliding merrily on, we come to Bedford station, at which place the guard-house, about two stories high, commands a good view of the tracks in all directions; being in charge of trustworthy operators especially selected for this important post, where a cool head and great presence of mind are necessary in order to avoid any and all accidents which might otherwise arise from a misplaced switch, etc. Here the road curves to the right, and runs directly toward the island.

As we whirl along we catch glimpses of charming bits of scenery, romantic woodlands and groves, beautiful flower gardens, elegant and substantial homes, and some of the finest market gardens the State contains.

We pass the beautiful villages of Flatbush, Parkville, Gravesend, and stop a moment at Sheepshead Bay, the last station and village before we come to the island. Crossing the small creek which separates Coney Island from Long Island, we notice at our right the Brighton Beach Racing Course, and in two or three seconds we arrive at the depot.

During the summer 57 trains run each way daily over this road, but on holidays the number is materially increased. The cars of this line are beautifully finished, the engines large and powerful, and the entire rolling stock as good as any that runs to the beach, with trains rarely or never a moment late. We notice the employees as being very polite and attentive, especially to ladies and children, and also using every precaution for the safety and comfort of passengers.

Passing through the depot, we enter the

BRIGHTON BEACH HOTEL.

This magnificent structure is under the management of Mr. Chas. E. Leland, a gentleman whose reputation is not confined within local limits, and whose success as a manager of some of the best known of American hotels has been something phenomenal. Mr. Leland has conducted the world-wide known Delavan House at Albany, the Clarendon, and Rossmore Hotels of New York City, with unprecedented success, and now enters a new

Kranich & Bach's Grand, Square and Upright **Pianos,**
On Monthly Installments, A. G. SLADE, Brooklyn Agent, 593 Fulton St.

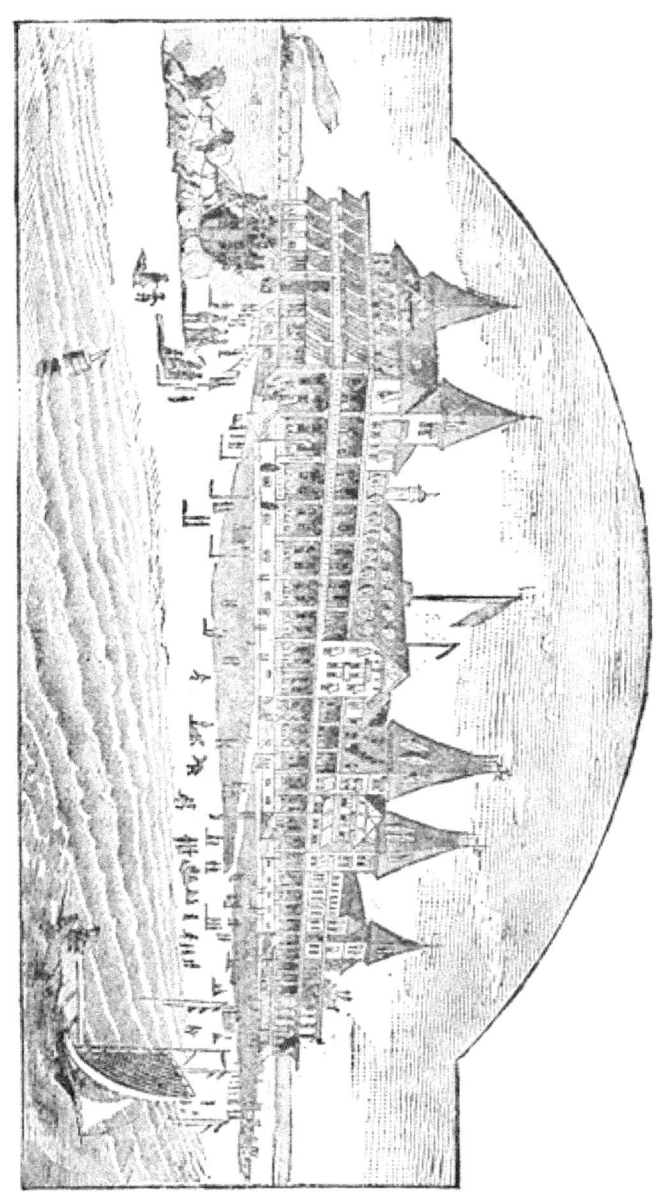

Hotel Brighton, Brighton Beach, Coney Island.

field of labor at the Hotel Brighton, Brighton Beach, and proposes to make it one of the finest hotels in the country.

The entire structure has been remodeled, renovated and redecorated from top to bottom, and contains 300 rooms, the greater part of which have been newly furnished, with elegant accommodations for 600 permanent guests, and affords the seclusion and quietude of a family hotel of the first order, the entire upper floors being reserved exclusively for the use of permanent guests, with broad piazzas on each side of the hotel, affording a splendid view of the sea and of the highly cultivated country visible from the rear of the building.

Fronting the hotel, the grounds are beautifully and tastefully laid out in flower beds, which form an enchanting picture, strongly in contrast with the monotonous white sand. This hotel is the principal point of attraction at this portion of the beach. Directly opposite the main entrance of the hotel is the music stand, around which are ranged seats for a large number of people. The instrumental concerts of the Brighton Beach Hotel are largely attractive. The best musical talent has always been engaged, and will be furnished this season by the celebrated BALLENBERG'S Band, of Cincinnati, every afternoon and evening. The musical feast, furnished free, in itself induces a very large attendance, which, upon frequent occasions, is still further augmented by a liberal display of pyrotechnics. Indeed, the superior quality of the music and the artistic fireworks exhibitions constitute in no small measure the popularity of Brighton Beach.

At night, when illuminated with Chinese lanterns, the grounds of the hotel present a surpassingly beautiful appearance, and the animation and gaiety everywhere prevailing lend increased attractiveness to the scene. The dining-rooms of the hotel will seat 1,500 people, and the *cuisine* facilities are such that 10,000 guests may be fed here daily. As we leave the hotel steps we are astonished at the change since last season. "Old Neptune" having encroached to such an extent, rendered it necessary to move the Bathing Pavilion farther inland, until now it stands almost in line with the hotel, while at other portions of the beach the ocean has receded.

The Pharmacy building, recently refitted and now under the supervision of Jas. Morgan, M. D., presents a very attractive

Kranich & Bach's Grand, Square and Upright Pianos,

On Monthly Installments, A. G. SLADE, Brooklyn Agent, 593 Fulton St.

BRIGHTON BEACH BATHING PAVILION, CONEY ISLAND.

appearance as we approach the Pavilion. The immense fountain, brought here from the Centennial Exposition at Philadelphia, stands in the centre of the store, the admiration of all visitors. The store contains all kinds of drugs and fancy articles, such as usually found at any first-class druggist's; and the prescription department is open day and night, and all medicines carefully compounded by none but experienced hands. Arrangements are made whereby Dr. Morgan (for the past four years physician at Brighton Hotel) can be summoned at any hour from the store by telephone connecting with his residence at Sheepshead Bay.

Entering the Pavilion, we are attracted by a large gathering of people to the Brighton Silk Works, located here for several years past. Mr. Henry Mitchell, the proprietor, directed our attention to a patent appliance invented since last season, which may be attached to any silk power loom, and capable of weaving patterns of flowers or ornaments of most any design or color in silk. Many thousand dollars have been expended in trying to perfect this important improvement, but all to no purpose, until, accidentally, through Mr. Mitchell, this simple contrivance was discovered.

We see all manner of articles exposed for sale. Also, the famous "Silhouettes," on black paper. "Cut your profile while you wait," pails and shovels; "try your weight; "have your fortune told;" "test your nerves on this electric battery," etc.

We enter the office of the Brighton Improvement Company (Limited), and are met by Mr. John Y. Fitchett, general manager, a gentleman of sterling qualities and rare abilities, long connected with the company in this capacity, and faithful to his trust. Said he, to our queries:

"The syndicate forming this company are composed of five very wealthy gentlemen, who receive large dividends from moneys invested. The Bathing Pavilion is 490 feet long. We have 1,230 bathing rooms on the second floor, and have often accommodated over 6,000 bathers in one day. We require, and have 12,000 suits for both sexes, and 30,000 towels. Two bridges lead to the beach from the bath-rooms. Besides this, we have 16 hot water bathing-rooms in the building, elaborately fitted with imported porcelain tubs, costing over $1,500 each; the plumbing work of course forming one of the greatest items, and consisting of over three miles of pipe if laid in a straight line.

"Our laundry is very extensive, having cost $20,000 ; we have ninety-three steam dryers and ten large centrifugal wringers. After bathers lay aside their suits, they are gathered up, thrown into a car which, when filled, is dumped into a sluice-way, leading to a large vat filled with water ; here the suits are washed, taken from the water, dried by steam, and again on the shelf inside of twenty minutes."

"We use in illuminating the pavilion thirteen electric lights and over 8,000 gas jets. The company own their own gas works, and upon the entire Brighton property there is consumed over 55,000 feet of gas per night ; 2,500 tons of coal are consumed in four months."

"What a vast amount of money must be required to run such an establishment," said "Joe."

"You may form some idea of the expense," said Mr. Fitchett, "When I tell you, that when we are fully equipped, in addition to what I have already said, we employ upwards of 700 employees, with salary and board, ranging from $15 to $175 per month."

"Tad," in a thoughtful mood, said :

> "How great the imaginative power
> Of man, when in an obvious hour,
> To erect such structures on the land
> Of Coney Island's glist'ning strand."
>
> "Here's sport for all, the low and great,
> Where bipeds splash in every shape ;
> The parent, child and artful maid,
> Have sung its praise through one decade."

"See," said "Joe," looking through the open door, "What throngs of people are continually passing ! " Then to the general manager, "About how many people are estimated as crossing this pavilion daily ? "

"The number is in excess of 20,000, this being the only avenue between the two great corporations of Brighton and Manhattan."

Leaving the office, our eyes are caught by a conspicuous sign, bearing the inscription :

"Bunnell's cool pleasure, Brighton Museum."
Said "Tad:"

"Let's step into BUNNELL'S an hour to beguile,
'Tis the worthiest show on all Coney Isle.
Here strange freaks of nature, from various part
Of this and the old world, may knowledge impart."

We enter the museum during exhibition of the living curiosities; and the first person we recognize in the large gathering is MR. BUNNELL, so well and popularly known in New York and Brooklyn, as a gentleman having attained the highest standing in his profession. During the past years he has introduced, to the people of our great cities, some of the greatest living wonders of the world, and as an *honest showman* he stands as one without a superior. We give below a faithful bust picture of

G. B. BUNNELL.

Kranich & Bach's Grand, Square and Upright Pianos,

On Monthly Installments, A. G. SLADE, Brooklyn Agent, 593 Fulton St

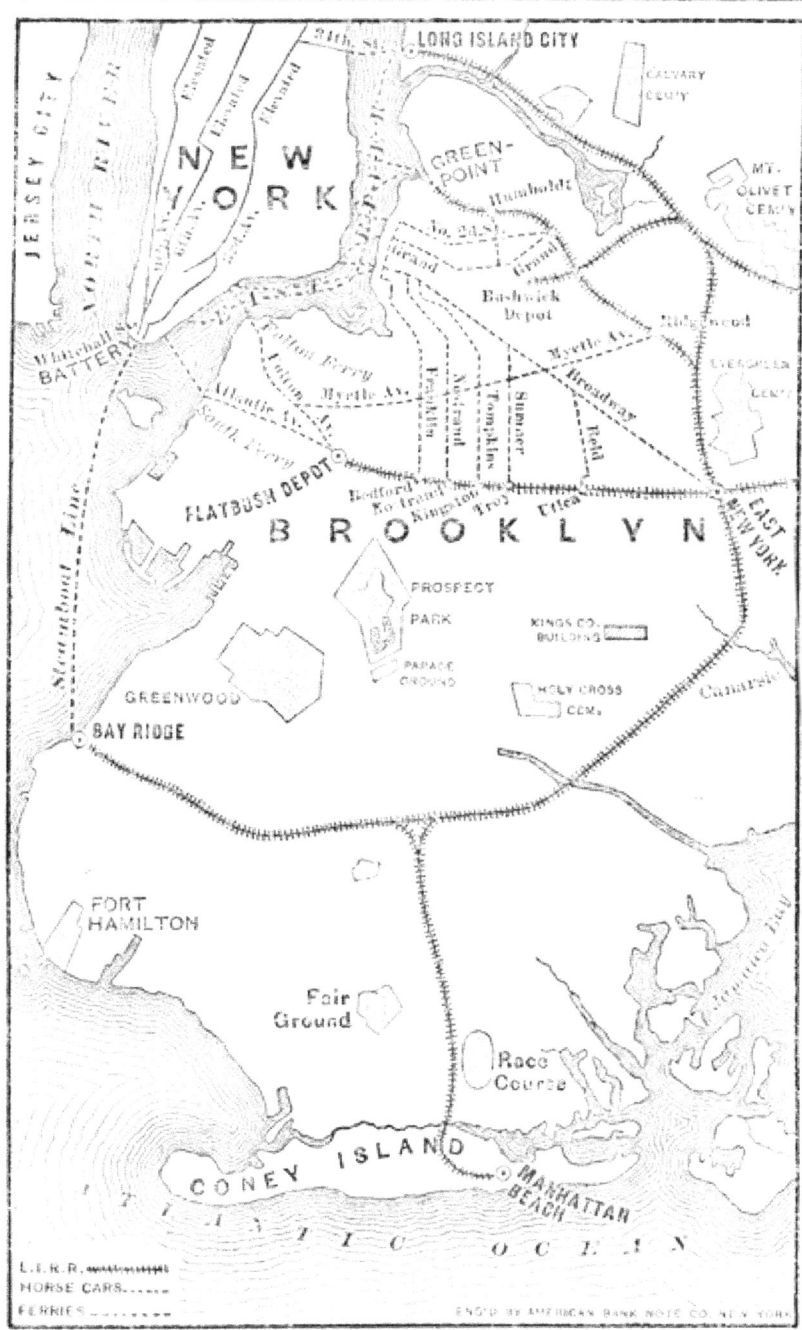

MANHATTAN BEACH RAILWAY MAP.

While listening to the introduction, history, modes of living, etc., of the various persons and objects on exhibition, we were greatly enlightened, as one after another claimed our attention.

Especially so when in conversation with Miss Nellie Walker, the "Albino" lady, who said, "I was born in Paterson, N. J.; my parents before me were also born there. I am not a "*Madagascar*," or "*Moorish*" lady. I am now twenty years of age; when my mother died I was but five and a half years old; since then I have been on exhibition. An *Albino* is only a *peculiar freak of nature*."

Next we see "Dahoma," the giant from Jacksonville, Ohio, measuring seven feet eleven inches high, and weighing 225 lbs., a very pleasant and agreeable gentleman. "Richard James," the fat boy, born in Wayne county, Ohio; 19 years old, weighs 504 lbs , 5 feet, 9 inches high, 69 inches around the chest, and 73 inches around the waist; and many other attractions. "Tad" said :

> "Here giants and midgets enliven the shows,
> A boy without arms that can write with his toes.
> A fair Indian princess, we'll name not her age,
> Who came from the far frozen land of OSAGE.
> Here the brown HINDOO lady that's ne'er known to fail
> When her husband's away to conceal with her vail
> Those features, which may not seem lovely to you,
> Yet lovely when seen by a heathen HINDOO.
> Now BUNNELL, STARR, WHISTON in order we'll name,
> A trio, or triplet, it means just the same.
> Each cater to *please you*, and *happiness* bring ;
> This power in showman we think just the thing."

Leaving Bunnell's Museum we enter the station of the Marine Railway, running to Manhattan Beach. This road has been rebuilt the whole distance on piles, thus allowing ingress and egress to the waves, and making travel possible in all weathers.

MANHATTAN BEACH

possesses more than two miles of sea front, fringed by a fine sandy beach, whose beautiful curves wind in and out, and upon which unceasingly rolls the majestic surf. To stand upon this beach and look over the vast expanse of water, shut out only by the horizon, is a view of itself sufficient to repay one for visiting

Kranich & Bach's Grand, Square and Upright Pianos,

On Monthly Installments, A. G. SLADE, Brooklyn Agent, 593 Fulton St.

Manhattan Beach Hotel, Coney Island.

the resort. The great Atlantic Ocean is spread before the gaze, making a marine picture of unparalleled beauty.

Turning from the ocean and looking toward the land, a view of no less beauty, but of a different kind, attracts the eye. Laid out in the landscape gardener's most exquisite taste, are extensive walks, lawns and flower beds. The walks are broad, and as clean as the most private of gardens. The lawns are like patches of green velvet, and the flower-beds are kaleidoscopic with the bloom of choicest plants.

Fronting this, stand the hotels and pavilions, separated by the same walks and lawns, which surround them on all sides. Beyond, seen through the opening, is Sheepshead Bay, and still further beyond are the sloping shores of the mainland, with its dottings of foliage and picturesque cottages. All this forms a picture worthy the attention of the most skillful artist, and the admiration of the most ardent sight-seer.

The facilities for reaching this great seaside resort are unsurpassed, and the time spent in transit, but 32 minutes from the L. I. R. R. Depot, junction of Flatbush and Atlantic avenues, direct to the beach without change of cars, and is easily reached by horse cars, running directly from Catharine, Fulton, Wall and South Ferries. Fare for the round trip, only 25 cents. The Greenpoint Division connects with trains from Long Island City at Cooper avenue junction, intersecting the various horse railroads, and winds thence through a rich garden country, which extends veritably to the ocean. Also by steamboat from Whitehall slip, terminus of the East and West Side Elevated Railway, to Bay Ridge, and thence by the New York and Manhattan Beach Railway; or by the all-rail route from Long Island City, via, Thirty-fourth street, Seventh street and James slip Ferries, Annex Boats from Pier 17, E. R., and Greenpoint, Brooklyn, opposite Tenth and Twenty-third street ferries, direct to the Beach. Both these routes, as they near the beach, converge and terminate at the rear of the hotels. All the roads are broad-gauge, except the Greenpoint branch, which is a narrow-gauge, and transfers passengers at Cooper avenue junction.

The initial building connected with the enterprise is the Manhattan Beach Hotel. This hotel is peculiarly adapted to the

Kranich & Bach's Grand, Square and Upright Pianos,

On Monthly Installments, A. G. SLADE, Brooklyn Agent, 593 Fulton St.

Oriental Hotel, Manhattan Beach, Coney Island.

wants of transient guests, for whose convenience its spacious piazzas, commodious parlors, and extensive rooms on the first floor are offered. All above the first floor is reserved for permanent sojourners, who can have all the enjoyments of the place, without mingling with the crowd.

"The Oriental Hotel" was erected in the spring of 1880, and opened for business during the summer. In building the "Oriental" particular reference was had to the needs of families, the aim being to have it as retired as possible, where a household could live in a body, be quiet and secluded, and yet be within reach of the livelier attractions if desired. As a seaside hotel the "Oriental" surpasses anything of its kind. Its exterior is unique and very imposing, and its interior is finished to perfection. It has large rooms furnished without regard to cost, and possesses an elevator for the convenience of guests. It is provided with steam apparatus for heating, when necessary, and, like its sister hostelry, is lit by gas.

Besides these establishments, there are the great Pavilion for excursion and picnic parties, and the Bathing Pavilion situated between the two hotels. The Bathing Pavilion is provided with every convenience, and all necessary appliances used and precautions taken to insure the lives of bathers; notwithstanding the Beach is one of the safest in the world. No better beach for bathing purposes can be found on Coney Island than here at the Mammoth Bathing Pavilion, and with greater facilities for bathers in every respect than any place on the Atlantic coast. Nearly all trains start from and arrive at the rear of the "Oriental Hotel."

The lessee of the hotels and pavilion is Mr. J. H. Breslin, proprietor of the Gilsey House, N. Y., and the Southern Hotel, St. Louis, Mo., whose experience in catering for the public renders him thoroughly competent to satisfactorily meet the demands made upon him. Go where you will, in this country or in Europe, no better *cuisine* is found, and no better attendance given, than that at Manhattan Beach. Mr. Breslin's arrangements for guests are second to none. Provision is made, equally, for those whose purses can afford all the delicacies which money can command, and for those who are obliged to consult economy.

Mr. T. H. Ryan, the "Press Agent" of the Long Island Railroad, is again the lessee of the news stand at this point, and will evidently study the convenience of the guests as he has done for the past five years.

The "Bombardment of Alexandria," invented and produced by "Pain," of London, is a magnificent naval and military spectacle, prepared in England at great expense, and exhibited every Tuesday, Thursday and Saturday evenings during the season.

The picture representing the City and Harbor of ALEXANDRIA has been splendidly painted by Mr. Walter Mills and assistants, from sketches taken by Mr. Milton Prior, special artist of the "Illustrated London News," and other authentic authorities.

It is the intention of the management to reproduce the various incidents that led up to and took place during this memorable bombardment, including the massacre of the Europeans, the Admiral's demand, drilling of the troops, bombardment of the city by the English fleet, also its sacking and burning, landing of the English sailors and soldiers to quell the rioters, assisted by the Americans, marines, etc., for which purpose about three hundred and fifty men have been thoroughly drilled by "Col. Denslow," U. S. A., and fully equipped to represent the various combatants, soldiers, sailors, Arabs, etc.

After witnessing this fine illustration of the "Bombardment of ALEXANDRIA," we board the train at the depot of the Marine Railway which runs to Brighton. "Tad" tells it thus:

> "Now westward to Brighton by railway we speed,
> And then by a coach that is drawn by a steed;
> We move to West Brighton, the place of "Paul Bauer,"
> Of "Culver" and "Van" and the great "Iron Tower."
>
> "Hark! voices of gladness around me are ringing,
> The wild, joyous shout has now reached to a yell,
> Round, round the great circle all ages are swinging,
> And taking a ride on the great carrosselle."

This "Iron Tower" has been open to the public since 1878, during which time it has been under the superintendency of the gentlemanly and watchful "John L." No accident has ever occurred to either visitor or employee. This same gentleman is manager of the neat little carrosselle near the "Brighton Pier," as well as the Græco-Roman carrosselle directly south of the Observatory.

This is the most magnificent and most perfect in all its appointments of any in the known world, and the manifest appreciation of the public is a guarantee of its success.

Nothing more remains for us, reader, than to ask you to test the truth of what we have said in our " Ramble on the Beach."

" Tad," in leaving our party, becomes quite pathetic. He says :

"Friends of my pleasant stroll the lamps are fading !
   The surf rolls heavy on the sandy beach ;
Drear seem the great hotels, and few are trading ;
   Dense crowds are jostling the cars to reach.
The "last boat" now her crowded deck is lading
   With human freight—the locomotives screech !
Haste to the nearest seat in boat or car ;
Then speed we homeward from Coney afar.

"And if my boon companions, doomed no more
   To greet at either boat or railway station ;
To meet again on Coney Island's shore,
   And spend the day in pleasant recreation ;
To brave the surf, to hear the billows roar !
   Adieu !—now listen to my *last* narration :—
Should I no more *on earth* return thy *smile*,
In dreams we'll meet on happy Coney Isle.

NEW YORK AND BROOKLYN BRIDGE.

DESCRIPTION.

Construction commenced Jan. 3, 1870.
Size of New York caisson, 172x102 feet.
Size of Brooklyn caisson, 168x102 feet.
Timber and iron in caisson, 5,253 cubic yards.
Concrete in well holes, chambers, etc., 5,669 cubic feet.
Weight of New York caisson, about 7,000 tons.
Weight of concrete filling, 8,000 tons.
New York tower contains 46,945 cubic yards masonry.
Brooklyn tower contains 38,214 cubic yards masonry.
Length of river span, 1,595 feet 6 inches.
Length of each land span, 930 feet, 1,860 feet.
Length of Brooklyn approach, 971 feet.
Length of New York approach, 1,562 feet 6 inches.
Total length of bridge, 5,989 feet.
Width of bridge, 85 feet.
Number of cables, 4.
Diameter of each cable, 15¾ inches.
First wire was run out May 29, 1877.
Cable making really commenced June 11, 1877.
Length of each single wire in cables, 3,579 feet.
Length of wire in four cables, exclusive of wrapping wire, 14,361 miles.
Weight of four cables, inclusive of wrapping wire, 3,538½ tons.
Ultimate strength of each cable, 12,200 tons.
Weight of wire, nearly 11 feet per pound.
Each cable contains 5,296 parallel, not twisted, galvanized steel oil-coated wires, closely wrapped to a solid cylinder 15¾ inches in diameter.
Depth of tower foundation below high water, Brooklyn, 45 feet.
Depth of tower foundation below high water, New York, 78 feet.
Size of towers at high water line, 140x59 feet.
Size of towers at roof course, 136x53 feet.
Total height of towers above high water, 278 feet.
Clear height of bridge in centre of river span above high water at 90 degrees F., 135 feet.
Height of floor at towers above high water, 119 feet 3 inches.
Grade of roadway, 3¾ feet in 100 feet.
Height of towers above roadway, 159 feet.
Size of anchorages at base, 129x119 feet.
Size of anchorages at top, 117x104 feet.
Height of anchorages, 89 feet front, 85 feet rear.
Weight of each anchor plate, 23 tons.
Engineer, Col. W. A. Roebling.

NELSON & HOLDEN, **COAL.** Main Office, Degraw Street, on Gowanus Canal.

CONEY ISLAND.

West Brighton Beach, Brighton Beach, Manhattan Beach, Prospect Park and Coney Island Railroad.

EXCURSION TICKETS, 25 CENTS.

Including Admission to the New Brighton Pier.

PROSPECT PARK AND CONEY ISLAND R. R.

West Brighton Beach Division.

SUMMER TIME TABLE.

In effect from Sunday, June 19 to Sunday, Sept. 9, 1883, inclusive.

TRAINS FROM BROOKLYN

Leave Greenwood Depot, 9th Av. and 20th Street:

At *6.00, *7.00, 8.00, 9.00, 9.30, 10.00, 10.20, 10.40, 11.00, 11.20, 11.40 A.M.; 12.00 M.; 12.20, 12.40, 1.00, 1.15, 1.30, 1.45, 2.00, 2.15, 2.30, 2.45, 3.00, 3.15, 3.30, 3.45, 4.00, 4.15, 4.30, 4.45, 5.00, 5.15, 5.30, 5.45, 6.00, 6.15, 6.30, 6.45, 7.00, 7.15, 7.30, 7.45, 8.00, 8.15, 8.30, 8.45, 9.00, 9.15, 9.30, 9.45, 10.00, 10.15, 10.30, 10.45 P.M.

TRAINS FROM WEST BRIGHTON BEACH

Leave West Brighton Beach, Coney Island, for Greenwood Depot:

At *6.30, *7.30, 8.30, 9.30, 9.55, 10.25, 10.45, 11.05, 11.25, 11.45, A.M.; 12.05, 12.25, 12.45, 1.15, 1.30, 1.45, 2.00, 2.15, 2.30, 2.45, 3.00, 3.15, 3.30, 3.45, 4.00, 4.15, 4.30, 4.45, 5.00, 5.15, 5.30, 5.45, 6.00, 6.15, 6.30, 6.45, 7.00, 7.15, 7.30, 7.45, 8.00, 8.15, 8.30, 8.45, 9.00, 9.15, 9.30, 9.45, 10.00, 10.15, 10.30, 10.45, 11.00, 11.15 P.M.

* Do not run on Sundays.

All Excursion Tickets issued by the Iron Steamboat Co. at New York are good to return over the road of this Company, and all horse car lines running from its Brooklyn Depot to Hamilton, South, Wall, Fulton and Catharine Ferries.

☞ "VARIATIONS" from this Time Table will only be made on "RAINY DAYS," and as "CIRCUMSTANCES" and the "PUBLIC CONVENIENCE" may require.

NELSON & HOLDEN, COAL. Main Office, Degraw Street, on Gowanus Canal.

New York and Sea Beach Railway.

Connecting with Steamers "Sylvan Dell," "Sylvan Stream," and "Sylvan Grove," and on Sundays "Chrystenah" additional.

Summer (Daily) Time Table, 1883.

Boats Leave West 23d St. N. R.

At 9.00, 9.40, 10.20, 11 00, 11.40, A. M., and 12.20, 1.00, 1.40, 2.20, 3.00, 3.40, 4.20, 5.00, 5.40, 6.20, 7 00, 7.40, 8.20 and 9 P. M.

Boats Leave Pier 6, N. R.

At 8.25, 9.25, 10.05, 10.45, 11.25 A. M., and 12.05, 12.45, 1.25, 2.05, 2.45, 3.25, 4.05, 4.45, 5.25, 6.05, 6.45, 7.25 and 8.05 P. M.

Leaves Bay Ridge Landing

At 7.00, 7.40, 8.50, 9.50, 10.10, 10.30, 11.10, 11.50, A. M., and 12.30, 1.10, 1.30, 1.50, 2.10, 2.30, 2.50, 3.10, 3.30, 3.50, 4.10, 4.30, 4.50, 5.10, 5.30, 5.50, 6.10, 6.30, 6.50, 7.10, 7.30, 7.50, 8.10, 8.30, 8.50, 9.10, 9.30, 9.50 and 10.10 P. M.

Leaves Coney Island for Bay Ridge

At 7.35, 8.30, 9.30, 10.15 10.35, 10.55, 11.35, A. M., and 12.15, 12.55, 1.35, 1.55, 2.15, 2.35, 2.55, 3.15, 3.35, 3.55, 4.15, 4.35, 4.55, 5.15, 5.35, 5.55, 6.15, 6.35, 6.55, 7.15, 7.35, 7.55, 8.15, 8.35, 8.55, 9.15, 9.35, 9.55, 10.15 and 10.45 P. M.

Leaves Coney Island for Pier 6 and West 23d St. N. R.

At 7.35, 8.30, 9.30, 10.15, 10.55, 11.35, A. M., and 12.15, 12.55, 1.35, 2.15, 2.55, 3.35, 4.15, 4.55, 5.35, 6.15, 6.55, 7.35, 8.15, 8.55, 9.35 and 10.15 P. M.

Sunday Time Table, July and August, 1883.

Leaves Bay Ridge

At 8.30, 9.20, 9.40, 10.05, 10.30, 10.45, 11.00, 11.15, 11.30, 11.45. A. M.; 12 M. and 12.15, 12.30, 12.45, 1.00, 1.15, 1.30, 1.45, 2.00, 2.15, 2.30, 2.50, 3.10, 3 30, 3.50, 4.10, 4.30, 4.50, 5.10, 5.30, 5.50, 6.10, 6.30, 6.50, 7.10, 7.30, 7.50, 8 10, 8.30, 8.50, 9.10, 9.30, 9.50 and 10.10 P. M.

Leaves Coney Island for Bay Ridge

At 9.00, 9.50, 10.10, 10.40, 10.55, 11.10, 11.25, 11.40, 11.55 A. M., and 12.10, 12.25, 12.40, 12.55, 1.10, 1.25, 1.40, 1.55, 2.10, 2.25, 2.40, 2.55, 3.15, 3.35, 3.55, 4.15, 4.35, 4.55, 5.15, 5.35, 5.55, 6.15, 6.35, 6.55, 7.15, 7.35, 7.55, 8.15, 8.35, 8.55, 9.15, 9.35, 9.55, 10.15 and 10.45 P. M.

Sundays,

Boats every half-hour from West 23d Street and Pier 6, N. R.

C. W. DOUGLAS, Superintendent.

PHOTOGRAPHS

IN THE LATEST AND MOST APPROVED STYLES.

Examine specimens and compare prices with other first-class work.

COPYING AND ENLARGING

In Crayon, Ink, Pastel, and Water Colors.

OILS A SPECIALTY.

Pictures taken equally as well on Cloudy Days.

DURYEA,

251 and 253 Fulton Street,

BROOKLYN.

NELSON & HOLDEN, COAL. Main Office, Degraw Street, on Gowanus Canal.

New York and Sea Beach Railway.

SUMMER TIME TABLE, 1883.

Leaves Third Av. Junction for Coney Island

At 7.03, 7.43, 8.53, 9.53, 10.13, 10.33, 11.13, 11.53, A. M., and 12.33, 1.13, 1.33, 1.53, 2.13, 2.33, 2.53, 3.13, 3.33, 3.53, 4.13, 4.33, 4.53, 5.13, 5.33, 5.53, 6.13, 6.33, 6.53, 7.13, 7.33, 7.53, 8.13, 8.34, 8.53, 9.13, 9.34, 9.53 and 10.13 P. M.

Leaves Coney Island for Third Av. Junction

At 7.35, 8.30, 9.30, 10.15, 10.35, 10.55, 11.15, 11.35, 11.55 A. M., and 12.15, 12.35, 12.55, 1.15, 1.35, 1.55, 2.15, 2.35, 2.55, 3.15, 3.35, 3.55, 4.15, 4.35, 4.55, 5.15, 5.35, 5.55, 6.15, 6.35, 6.55, 7.15, 7.35, 7.55, 8.15, 8.35, 8.55, 9.15, 9.35, 9.55, 10.15 and 10.45 P. M.

Special Sunday Time Table.

Leaves Third Av. Junction for Coney Island

At 8.33, 9.23, 9.43, 10.08, 10.33, 10.48, 11.03, 11.18, 11.33, 11.48 A. M., and 12.03, 12.18, 12.33, 12.48, 1.03, 1.18, 1.33, 1.48, 2.03, 2.18, 2.33, 2.53, 3.13, 3.33, 3.53, 4.13, 4.33, 4.53, 5.13, 5.33, 5.53, 6.13, 6.33, 6.53, 7.13, 7.33, 7.53, 8.13, 8.33, 8.53, 9.13, 9.33, 9.53, and 10.13. P. M.

Leaves Coney Island for Third Av. Junction

At 9.00, 9.50, 10.10, 10.40, 10.55, 11.10, 11.25, 11.40, 11.55, A. M., and 12.10, 12.25, 12.40, 12.55, 1.10, 1.25, 1.40, 1.55, 2.10, 2.25, 2.40, 2.55, 3.15, 3.35, 3.55, 4.15, 4.35, 4.55, 5.15, 5.35, 5.55, 6.15, 6.35, 6.55, 7.15, 7.35, 7.55, 8.15, 8.35, 8.55, 9.15, 9.35, 9.55, 10.15 and 10.45 P. M.

C. W. DOUGLAS, Superintendent.

MAGNETISM IS LIFE.

"WILSONIA"

Magnetic Appliances

Are the **marvel** of the world for the **cure** and relief of **disease without Medicine.**

All diseases that are curable, and some that are considered incurable, yield to its vitalizing influence.

Thousands that once were sick are to-day in the enjoyment of health, and they bear testimony that they were cured by

"WILSONIA" MAGNETIC APPLIANCES.

Special Appliances for **Tourists** and **Travelers**, to be worn as a safeguard against disease in all climates, are **indispensable.**

Illustrated Pamphlets containing full information, Testimonials and Price List mailed Free on application.

Office Hours, from 8 A. M. to 8 P. M. daily.

Consultations and all information free of charge. Orders and inquiries by Mail will receive prompt attention.

Original Office and Salesrooms,

465 FULTON ST., BROOKLYN, N. Y.

W. S. WINTERS, Agent.

N. B.—Beware of Fraudulent Imitations.

NELSON & HOLDEN, **COAL.** Main Office, Degraw Street, on Gowanus Canal.

Brooklyn, Bath and Coney Island
RAILWAY.
Summer Time Table, July 1, 1883.

Leaves Greenwood Depot

At 6.15, 7.14, 8.10. 9.00, 9.50. 10.40, 11.30, A. M.; 12.00, M., and 12.30, 1.00, 1.30, 2.00, 2.30, 3.00, 3.30, 4.00, 4.30, 5.00, 5.30, 6.00, 7.00, 7.30, 8.00, 8.30 9.20, 10.10, 11.00, 11.50, P. M.

Leaves Coney Island

At 7.00, 8.00, 9.00, 10.00, 10.50, 11.40, A. M., and 12.10, 12.40, 1.10, 1.40, 2.10, 2.40, 3.10, 3.40, 4.10, 4.40, 5.10, 5.40, 6.10, 6.40, 7.10, 7.40, 8.10, 8.40, 9.30, 10.20, 11.10, P. M.

SUNDAY TIME TABLE.

Leaves Greenwood Depot

At 8.10, 9.00, 9.50, 10.40, 11.30, A. M.; 12.00, M., and 12.30, 1.00, 1.20, 1.40, 2.00, 2.20, 2.40, 3.00, 3.20, 3.40, 4.00, 4.20, 4.40, 5.00, 5.20, 5.40, 6.00, 6.20, 6.40, 7.00, 7.20, 7.40, 8.00, 8.20, 8.40, 9.00, 9.20, 10.10, 11.00, 11.50, P. M.

Leaves Coney Island

At 7.00, 8.00, 9.00, 10.00, 10.50, 11.40, A. M., 12.10, 12.40, 1.20, 1.40, 2.00, 2.20, 2.40, 3.00, 3.20, 3.40, 4.00, 4.20, 4.40, 5.00, 5.20, 5.40, 6.00, 6.20, 6.40, 7.00, 7.20, 7.40, 8.00, 8.20, 8.40, 9.00, 9.30, 10.20, 11.10 P. M.

N. Y. & M. B. R. R. Connections—to New York.

Leave CONEY ISLAND at 8.00, 9.00 and 10 A. M.
Leave BATH 12 minutes later.

N. B.—The cars running from Fulton, South, Wall street and Hamilton avenue Ferries to Greenwood Cemetery, Main entrance, connect with this route.

POST

Yourself with my prices of
Sheet Music, Books, Pianos
ETC.

Songs of the Times. Gems of Song.
Popular Songs and Ballads.

Bound in Paper, 10c. each. **12c. by Mail.**

Song Folio, Folio of Music, Dance Folio, Mendelssohn Songs (without words).

Paper, 50c. each. **65c. by Mail.**

I also allow ¼ discount on all Sheet Music, and a liberal discount on Books.

Remember that I sell the **Hazelton Bros'. Pianos** lower for cash than any other dealer in the Union. The Hazelton Bros'. Pianos stand A No. 1 in every way.

Having been in the Music and Piano Business in this city for some 16 years (with a once leading firm), and having a thorough knowledge of the business, I can offer better inducements to my customers than any other dealer of this city. One visit to my establishment will convince you. When you wish anything in the line of Sheet Music, Pianos, etc., send direct to me.

Pianos and Organs Tuned and Repaired.

SAMUEL H. POST,
COR. FLATBUSH and LAFAYETTE AVS.

1 Block from the Long Island Depot.

NELSON & HOLDEN, COAL. Main Office, Degraw Street, on Gowanus Canal.

BRIGHTON BEACH,
Brooklyn, Flatbush and Coney Island Railway.

FLATBUSH DEPOT DIVISION.

On and after Friday, June 15, 1883, trains will be run as follows from Long Island Brighton Depot, junction of Flatbush and Atlantic avenues, stopping at Vanderbilt avenue and Prospect Park.

Leave Flatbush Avenue for Brighton

At 6.30, 7.15, 8.15, 9.15, 9.45, 10.15, 10.45, 11.15 and 11.45 A. M., and 12.15, 12.45, 1.15, 1.45, 2.15, 2.45, 3.15, 3.45, 4.15, 4.45, 5.15, 5.45, 6.15, 6.45, 7.15, 7.45, 8.15, 8.45, 9.15, 9.45, 10.15, 10.45, 11.15 and 11.45 P. M.

Returning, Leave Brighton Beach for Flatbush Av.

At 6.40, 7.40, 8.40, 9.40, 10.10, 10.40, 11.10, 11.40 and 11.55 A. M., and 12.10, 12.25, 12.40, 12.55, 1.10, 1.25, 1.40, 1.55, 2.10, 2.25, 2.40, 2.55, 3.10, 3.25, 3.40, 3.55, 4.10, 4.25, 4.40, 4.55, 5.10, 5.25, 5.40, 5.55, 6.10, 6.25, 6.40, 6.55, 7.10, 7.25, 7.40, 7.55, 8.10, 8.25, 8.40, 8.55, 9.10, 9.25, 9.40, 9.55, 10.10, 10.25, 10.40 and 11.10 P. M.

On Sundays first train for Brighton leaves at 8.15. Returning, leaves Brighton at 8.40.

ROBERT WHITE, Gen'l Superintendent.

CONCERTS at BRIGHTON BEACH every afternoon and evening by BALLENBERG'S BAND.

Flatbush Avenue depot is reached by Atlantic Street and Fifth Avenue cars, from Fulton, Wall and South Ferries, and by the Flatbush Avenue and Boerum Street cars from Fulton Ferry. Bedford station is reached by Franklin Avenue cars from Grand Street Ferry; Lafayette Avenue stages from Wall Street Ferry, and Rapid Transit trains. All trains to and from Flatbush Avenue stop at Vanderbilt Avenue to land and receive passengers. This Table may be varied from on unpleasant days. Cars pass the Flatbush Avenue depot for Fulton, Wall and South Ferries every two minutes. Close connections made with all Annex Boats at Fulton Ferry, from Jersey City, and all roads entering there; also the People's Line of Steamers, the Fall River Line, and Steamer Mary Powell. R. WHITE, Sup't.

Baggage at Hotels and Residences will be called for and delivered at Hotel Brighton, upon orders left at the offices of Westcott's Express Co., as follows:

NEW YORK, 3 Park Place; 785 Broadway, cor. 10th Street; 942 Broadway; Grand Central Depot, 42d Street; H. R. R. R. Depot, 30th Street, bet. 9th and 10th Avenues; Morris and Essex R. R. Depot, Barclay Street; Morris and Essex R. R. Depot, Christopher Street; Long Island R. R. Depot, James Slip; Long Island R. R. Depot, 34th Street, E. R.

BROOKLYN, 333 Washington Street, City Hall Square.

WILLIAMSBURGH, 79 Fourth Street, one door east of Broadway.

JERSEY CITY, 261 Warren Street.

HOBOKEN, Morris and Essex R. R. Depot.

CARR & MURRAY,

LEADING

Carpet, Furniture,

And Bedding House in Brooklyn.

Moquette Carpets,	-	from $1 25	per yard.
Body Brussels,	- -	" 1 00	"
Tapestry Carpets,	-	" 57	"
Ingrain "	- -	" 30	"
Oil Cloths,	- - -	" 25	"
Linoleum,	- - - -	75	"
Window Shades,	-	from 30	each.
Mattings,	- - - -	" 12½	per yd.
Parlor Furniture,	- -	" 25 00	a Set up
Bed-room Furniture,	-	" 16 00	"

With an elegant line of other fine goods at equally low prices. Give us a call.

CARR & MURRAY,

Nos. 61 AND 63 MYRTLE AVENUE,

3d Door West of Jay St.,   **BROOKLYN.**

NELSON & HOLDEN, **COAL.** Main Office, Degraw Street, on Gowanus Canal.

BRIGHTON BEACH,
Brooklyn, Flatbush and Coney Island Railway.

BEDFORD DIVISION.

On and after Friday, June 15, 1883, trains will be run as follows from Bedford Station:

Leave Bedford for Brighton

At 6.35, 7.20, 8.20, 9.20, 9.50, 10.20, 10.50 and 11.34 A. M., and 12.04, 12.34, 1.04, 1.34, 2.04, 2.34, 3.04, 3.34, 4.04, 4.34, 5.04, 5.34, 6.04, 6.34, 7.04, 7.34, 8.04, 8.34, 9.04, 9.34, 10.04, 10.30, 10.50, 11.00, 11.20 and 11.50 P. M.

Returning, Leave Brighton Beach for Bedford

At 6.40, 7.40, 8.40, 9.40, 10.10, 10.40, 11.10, 11.40 and 11.55 A. M., and 12.10, 12.25, 12.40, 12.55, 1.10, 1.25, 1.40, 1.55, 2.10, 2.25, 2.40, 2.55, 3.10, 3.25, 3.40, 3.55, 4.10, 4.25, 4.40, 4.55, 5.10, 5.25, 5.40, 5.55, 6.10, 6.25, 6.40, 6.55, 7.10, 7.25, 7.40, 7.55, 8.10, 8.25, 8.40, 8.55, 9.10, 9.25, 9.40, 9.55, 10.10, 10.25, 10.40 and 11.10 P. M.

On Sundays first train for Brighton leaves at 8.20. Returning, leaves Brighton at 8.40.

ROBERT WHITE, Gen'l Superintendent.

Concerts at Brighton Beach every afternoon and evening by

BALLENBERG'S BAND OF CINCINNATI.

Bedford Station is reached by horse-cars of the Vanderbilt Av. Line, and the Lee and Nostrand Av. Lines direct from Grand and Roosevelt St. Ferries; also from Hamilton Av. Ferry via Bergen St. cars.

R. WHITE, Sup't.

Baggage at Hotels and Residences will be called for and delivered at Hotel Brighton upon orders left at the offices of Westcott's Express Co. as follows:

NEW YORK, 3 Park Place; 785 Broadway, cor. 10th Street; 942 Broadway; Grand Central Depot, 42d Street; H. R. R. R. Depot, 30th Street, bet. 9th and 10th Avenues; Morris & Essex R. R. Depot, Barclay Street; Morris & Essex R. R. Depot, Christopher Street; Long Island R. R. Depot, James Slip; Long Island R. R. Depot, 34th Street, E. R.

BROOKLYN, 333 Washington Street, City Hall Square.
WILLIAMSBURGH, 79 Fourth Street, one door east of Broadway.
JERSEY CITY, 261 Warren Street.
HOBOKEN, Morris & Essex R. R. Depot.

HORATIO S. STEWART,

Real Estate and Insurance Broker,

No. 6 FOURTH AVENUE,

Bet. Flatbush and Atlantic Avs.,　　　　　　　BROOKLYN.

HOUSES LET AND RENTS COLLECTED

Money Loaned on Bond and Mortgage.

Special Attention Paid to the Management of Property.

Orders Received for Coal and Wood.

HENRY AFFEL.

DEALER IN

Choice Groceries, Teas

COFFEES, SPICES, Etc.

1169 BROADWAY, Corner Magnolia Street.

N. B.—All Orders Promptly Attended to.

NELSON & HOLDEN, **COAL.** Main Office, Degraw Street, on Gowanus Canal.

BRIGHTON BEACH,
Brooklyn, Flatbush and Coney Island Railway.

PROSPECT PARK DIVISION.

On and after Friday, June 15, 1883, trains will be run as follows from Prospect Park.

Leave Prospect Park Depot

At 6.40, 7.25, 8.25, 9.25, 9.55, 10.25, 10.55, 11.23, 11.38 and 11.53 A. M., and 12.09, 12.24, 12.39, 12.54, 1.10, 1.24, 1.39 1.54, 2.09, 2.24, 2.39, 2.54, 3.09, 3.24, 3.39, 3.54, 4.09, 4.24, 4.39, 4.54, 5.09, 5.24, 5.39, 5.54, 6.09, 6.24, 6.39, 6.54, 7.09, 7.24, 7.39, 7.54, 8.09, 8.24, 8.39, 8.54, 9.09, 9.24, 9.39, 9.55, 10.09, 10.25, 10.35, 10.55, 11.05, 11.25 and 11.55 P. M.

Returning, Leave Brighton Beach for Flatbush Av.

At 6.40, 7.40, 8.40, 9.40, 10.10, 10.40, 11.10, 11.40 and 11.55 A. M., and 12.10, 12.25, 12.40, 12.55, 1.10, 1.25, 1.40, 1.55, 2.10, 2.25, 2.40, 2.55, 3.10, 3.25, 3.40, 3.55, 4.10, 4.25, 4.40, 4.55, 5.10, 5.25, 5.40, 5.55, 6.10, 6.25, 6.40, 6.55, 7.10, 7.25, 7.40, 7.55, 8.10, 8.25, 8.40, 8.55, 9.10, 9.25, 9.40, 9.55, 10.10, 10.25, 10.40 and 11.10 P. M.

On Sundays first train for Brighton leaves at 8.25. Returning, leaves Brighton at 8.40.

Prospect Park is reached by Flatbush Avenue cars from Fulton Ferry; Lee and Nostrand Avenue cars, and Franklin Avenue cars from Grand and Roosevelt Street Ferries

ROBERT WHITE, Gen'l Superintendent.

Concerts at Brighton every afternoon and evening by **BALLENBERG'S BAND** of Cincinnati

Baggage at Hotels and Residences will be called for and delivered at Hotel Brighton upon orders left at the offices of Westcott's Express Co., as follows:

NEW YORK, 3 Park Place; 785 Broadway, cor. 10th Street; 942 Broadway; Grand Central Depot, 42d Street; H. R. R. R. Depot, 30th Street, bet. 9th and 10th Avenues; Morris and Essex R. R. Depot, Barclay Street; Morris and Essex R. R. Depot, Christopher Street; Long Island R. R. Depot, James Slip; Long Island R. R. Depot, 34th Street, E. R.

BROOKLYN, 333 Washington Street, City Hall Square.
WILLIAMSBURGH, 79 Fourth Street, one door east of Broadway.
JERSEY CITY, 261 Warren Street.
HOBOKEN, Morris and Essex R. R. Depot.

WESER BROS.

MANUFACTURERS OF

GRAND, SQUARE & UPRIGHT

PIANOS.

OFFICE AND PIANO FACTORY,

553, 555 AND 557 WEST 30th STREET,

PIANO CASE FACTORY,

413 AND 415 WEST 37th STREET,

NEW YORK.

N. B.—We Manufacture our own Cases, and therefore can safely recommend.

NELSON & HOLDEN, **COAL.** Main Office, Degraw Street, on Gowanus Canal.

IRON STEAMBOAT COMPANY.

THE ONLY ALL-WATER ROUTE DIRECT TO

CONEY ISLAND.

AND THE

GREAT IRON OCEAN PIERS, WEST BRIGHTON BEACH, BRIGHTON BEACH, MANHATTAN BEACH.

COOLEST, CLEANEST, SAFEST, AND QUICKEST ROUTES.

Leave Pier No. 1, North River,

Every forty minutes, for both Iron Piers and Coney Island Point, from 8.40 A. M. to 10.00 P. M. Returning

Leave Coney Island

From both Iron Piers and Coney Island Point, every forty minutes, from 8.00 A. M. to 11.15 P. M.

Take train at West Brighton Beach (Culver's) Depot for Coney Island Point Boats.

On Sundays and Holidays boats will be run half hourly.

EXCURSION TICKETS, 50 CENTS,
GOOD OVER ALL THE ROUTES.

Brighton Beach and Manhattan Beach are only ten minutes' walk from the Iron Piers and West Brighton Beach Depot, and are reached by Elevated Railroad, stages and carriages running in connection with the boats of this Company, continuously, day and evening.

FARE, 5 CENTS.

SPECIAL NOTICE.

The elevated railways have opened a new station at Battery Place, on Sixth and Ninth Avenue Lines, directly opposite the Iron Steamboat Company's Pavilion, Pier 1, North River. Passengers desiring to take boats, will leave the cars at that point.

Passengers from Second and Third Avenue Lines, holding Iron Steamboat excursion tickets, will be transferred to Sixth and Ninth Avenue Lines at South Ferry free.

Excursion Tickets for sale at all down-town track stations of the Elevated Railways, at 60 cents each.

HERMAN THIMIG'S Bottling Establishment,
50 BERGEN STREET. BROOKLYN.

Office, 288 Atlantic Av.,

CONEY ISLAND DEPOT, OCEAN PARKWAY,
near the Elevated Railroad.

Domestic and Imported Lager Beer, Ales, Porter,
CIDER, ETC., ETC.

Our well-known brands of Bottled Beer are sold at Brighton and Manhattan Beach, also at the two Iron Piers, Vanderveer's, Binder's, etc., etc.

NELSON & HOLDEN, **COAL.** Main Office, Degraw Street, on Gowanus Canal.

LONG ISLAND RAILROAD.

MANHATTAN BEACH DIVISION,

FROM

Flatbush Av. Depot, Brooklyn,

Direct to the Beach

WITHOUT CHANGE OF CARS.

SUMMER TIME TABLE.

Leave Flatbush Avenue Station

At †*7.20, 10.10, 11.10, 11.40 A. M., 12.10, 12.40, 1.10, 1.40, 2.10, 2.40, 3.10, †3.40, 4.10, †4.40, 5.10, †5.40, 6.10, 6.40, 7.10, 7.40, 8.10, 8.40, 9.10, 9.40 P. M.

Returning, Leave Manhattan Beach

At †*8.15, 11.00 A. M., 12.00 M, 12.25, 1.00, 1.25, 2.00, 2.25, 3.00, 3.25, 4.00, 4.25, †5.00, 5.25, †6.00, 6.25, 7.00, 7.25, 8.00, 8.25, 9.00, 9.25, 10.00, 10.40, P. M.

* Do not run on Sundays.

† Leave one minute from Oriental Hotel before Manhattan Beach time.

All Brooklyn Trains stop at BEDFORD, NOSTRAND, KINGSTON, TROY and UTICA AVENUE Stations going and returning.

Brooklyn Trains DO NOT stop at East New York.

This Company reserves the right to abandon any train on this table when found necessary.

Race Days all Trains Stop at Race Track During the Races.

I. D. BARTON,
 Gen'l Manager.

CHAS. M. HEALD,
 Gen'l Traffic Manager.

ILLUSTRATED GUIDE TO THE SEA.

The Philosopher

PHRENOLOGICAL
EXAMINATIONS,

The Humorist.

setting forth all the Strong and Weak points of character and disposition, showing clearly in each case what to Encourage and what to Restrain.

WILL AID YOUNG MEN

just starting in life who are full of Zeal, Strength and Courage in

SELECTING PROPER PURSUITS,

in which their abilities can be used to the best advantage, and their defects most effectually overcome, thus securing the best results of their efforts, and gaining honor and happiness.

YOUNG LADIES OF WEALTH AND LEISURE,

and their less fortunate sisters who must make their own way in the world, will find Phrenology an infallible guide to the proper use of their best powers.

PARENTS WILL BE SHOWN HOW

to understand and train turbulent, wayward, and selfish children, and how to bring their moral and intellectual powers into the ascendant; also how to deal with the delicate, tender and precocious so as

TO SECURE THE BEST RESULTS.

These examinations are given verbally and in Charts, with all the candor and faithfulness of confidential communications, and when desired,

FULL WRITTEN DESCRIPTIONS

are made, accompanied by a Book or Chart, with illustrations of the Organs, large and small, with full instructions how to cultivate and direct every faculty and emotion of the mind. Also,

DEFINITE SUGGESTIONS

as to who are, and who are not, adapted by temperament, constitution and disposition to be UNITED IN MARRIED LIFE, will be given daily at the

PHRENOLOGICAL CABINET,
753 BROADWAY, COR. 8th ST., NEW YORK,

where the large collection of Paintings, Casts, Busts and Skulls are on free exhibition.

CHARACTERS FROM LIKENESSES.

Those who cannot visit us in person, to obtain a PHRENOLOGICAL EXAMINATION, may send likenesses, if properly taken, and such measurements and description of complexion and general build, as to indicate Temperament.

Please send for circular called "Mirror of the Mind," which will explain what kind of likenesses are best for the purpose, and other particulars.

FOWLER & WELLS, Publishers,
No. 753 Broadway, New York.

NELSON & HOLDEN, **COAL.** Main Office, Degraw Street, on Gowanus Canal.

LONG ISLAND RAILROAD,

MANHATTAN BEACH DIVISION,

VIA BOAT FROM

WHITEHALL STREET,

TERMINUS OF ALL THE ELEVATED RAILWAYS,

AND

BAY RIDGE.

SUMMER TIME TABLE.

Leave New York

At 9.10, 10.10, 11.10 A. M., and 12.10, 1.10, 2.10, †3.10, †4.10, †5.10, 6.10, 7.10, 8.10 and 9.10 P. M.

Returning, Leave Manhattan Beach

At †*8.10, †5.10, 10.10, 11.10 A. M., and 12.10, 1.10, 2.10, 3.10, †4.10, †5.10, †6.10, 7.10, 8.10, 9.10 and 10.30 P. M.

* Do not run on Sunday.   † Do not stop at Sheepshead Bay.

Tickets by above route are good via Long Island City and East 34th Street Ferry.

Excursion tickets for sale at all down track stations of the Elevated Railways. Price, 60 cents, including Elevated Railway fares and Ferry, good either way via East 34th St. Ferry or Bay Ridge.

This Company reserves the right to abandon any train on this table when found necessary.

Race Days all Trains Stop at Race Track During the Races.

I. D. BARTON,   *CHAS. M. HEALD,*
  Gen'l Manager.   Gen'l Traffic Manager.

MANHATTAN BEACH HOTEL,

ORIENTAL HOTEL,

CONEY ISLAND,

J. H. BRESLIN.

GILSEY HOUSE,

BROADWAY,

NEW YORK CITY.

J. H. BRESLIN & BRO., Proprietors.

SOUTHERN HOTEL

COMPANY,

ST. LOUIS, MO.

J. H. BRESLIN, Proprietor.

NELSON & HOLDEN, **COAL.** Main Office, Degraw Street, on Gowanus Canal.

LONG ISLAND RAILROAD.

MANHATTAN BEACH DIVISION,
VIA
GREENPOINT,

TRANSFER AT COOPER AVENUE JUNCTION,

CONNECTING WITH

Through Trains from Long Island City.

SUMMER TIME TABLE.

Leave Greenpoint

At †*6.30, †8.40, 10.20, 11.20, 11.50 A. M., and 12.20, 12.50, 1.20, 1.50, 2.20, 2.50, 3.20, †3.50, 4.20, †4.50, 5.20, †5.50, 6.20, †6.50, 7.20, 7.50, 8.20, 8.50, 9.20 and 9.50 P. M.

Leave Humboldt st., 5 minutes, Grand st., 9 minutes, Ridgewood, 13 minutes after Greenpoint time, connecting at Cooper Avenue Junction with all Trains from Long Island City.

Returning, Leave Manhattan Beach

At †*7.35, †10.05, 11.20 A. M., and 12.20, 12.50, 1.20, 1.50, 2.20, 2.50, 3.20, 3.50, 4.20, †4.50, 5.20, †5.50, 6.20, †6.50, 7.20, 7.50, 8.20, 8.50, 9.20, 9.50, 10.20 and 10.50 P. M.

Connecting at Cooper Avenue Junction for Ridgewood, Grand, Humboldt and Greenpoint Stations.

* Do not run Sunday. † Do not stop at Sheepshead Bay.

This Company reserves the right to abandon any train on this table when found necessary.

Race Days all Trains Stop at Race Track During the Races.

J. D. BARTON,   CHAS. M. HEALD,
Gen'l Manager.   Gen'l Traffic Manager.

BRIGHTON PHARMACY,

Brighton Beach, Coney Island,

A FULL LINE OF FRESH

Pure Drugs and Chemicals

All Popular Pharmaceutical Preparations.

TOILET ARTICLES AND PERFUMERIES.

All Goods at Popular City Prices.

Soda and Mineral Water

Drawn from Tuft's Mammoth Arctic Mineral Spa.

PRESCRIPTIONS ACCURATELY COMPOUNDED

By Graduates in Pharmacy.

NELSON & HOLDEN, **COAL.** Main Office, Degraw Street, on Gowanus Canal.

LONG ISLAND RAILROAD.

MANHATTAN BEACH DIVISION,

VIA

34th St., 7th St., James Slip, and Annex Boats from foot of Pine St., East River,

AND

LONG ISLAND CITY.

SUMMER TIME TABLE.

Leave New York

At †*6.20, ‡8.30, 10.10, 11.10, 11.40 A. M., 12.10, 12.40, 1.10, 1.40, 2.10, 2.40, 3.10, ‡3.40, 4.10, ‡4.40, 5.10, ‡5.40, 6.10, 6.40, 7.00, 7.30, 8.00, 8.30, 9.00 and 9.30 P. M.

Leave Long Island City 10 minutes later.

Returning, Leave Manhattan Beach

At †7.35, ‡10.05, 11.20, A. M., and 12.20, 12.50, 1.20, 1.50, 2.20, 2.50, 3.20, 3.50, 4.20, ‡4.50, 5.20, ‡5.50, 6.20, ‡6.50, 7.20, 7.50, 8.20, 8.50, 9.20, 9.50, 10.20 and 10.50, P. M.

* Do not run on Sunday.   † Do not stop at Sheepshead Bay.

All the above trains stop at East New York.

Excursion tickets for sale at all down track stations of the Elevated Railways. Price, 60 cents, including Elevated Railway fares and Ferry, good either way via East 34th St. Ferry or Bay Ridge.

This Company reserves the right to abandon any train on this table when found necessary.

Race Days all Trains Stop at Race Track During the Races.

I. D. BARTON,   CHAS. M. HEALD,
  Gen'l Manager.   Gen'l Traffic Manager.

Mrs. Vanderveer's Hotel

AND

BATHING PAVILION,

CONCOURSE, TERMINUS P. P. & C. I. RAILROAD,

West Brighton Beach, Coney Island.

Best accommodations offered to permanent and transient guests.

MEALS ON THE EUROPEAN PLAN.

Rooms from $10 to $18 per week.

Superior accommodations are offered to families and permanent guests.

Ample shed room for driving parties.

Grounds illuminated by electric light.

The mammoth Bathing Pavilion is the finest and largest on the Beach.

Bathing Suits thoroughly cleaned.

Large Bar.

REFRESHMENTS SERVED

at both the Hotel and Bathing Pavilion.

NELSON & HOLDEN, **COAL.** Main Office, Degraw Street, on Gowanus Canal.

Coney Island by Horse Cars.

VIA JAY AND SMITH STS. AND HAMILTON AV. FERRY.

EXCURSION TICKETS, 20 CTS.

FROM FIFTEENTH STREET AND NINTH AVENUE.

Leave Fifteenth Street and Ninth Avenue

At 7.00, 8.00, 9.00, 9.40, 10.10, 10.40, 11.10, 11.40, A. M., and 12.20, 12.50, 1.20, 2.00, 2.30, 3.10, 3.40, 4.20, 4.50, 5.30, 6.00, 6.40, 7.10, 7.50, 8.20, 8.50, 9.30, P. M.

Leave Coney Island

At 6.00, 7.00, 8.00, 9.00, 10.00, 10.40, 11.10, 11.40, A. M., and 12.10, 12.50, 1.20, 2.00, 2.30, 3.10, 3.40, 4.20, 4.50, 5.30, 6.00, 6.40, 7.10, 7.50, 8.20, 9.10, P. M.

This line connects at Fifteenth street and Ninth avenue with cars to and from all the Brooklyn ferries.

June 11, 1883. *WM. FARRELL, Supt.*

STARIN'S GLEN ISLAND.

"It is as near fairyland, probably, as any place in this part of the world." —*N. Y. Times.*

AMERICA'S DAY SUMMER RESORT.   TWO GRAND CONCERTS DAILY.

Grafulla's Unrivaled Band,
Diller's Celebrated Cornet Quartet,
And Davis' Island Military Band.

DINNERS A LA CARTE.

OLD-FASHIONED RHODE ISLAND CLAM BAKE.
(Klein Deutschland.)
Bathing, Boating, Fishing, Bowling, Rifle Range, Billiards.

Glen Island Steamers leave at frequent intervals

**Pier 18, North River.   Jewell's Wharf, Brooklyn.
33d Street, East River.**

40 CENTS.   EXCURSION TICKETS.   40 CENTS.

For Time Table, See Daily Papers.

BRIGHTON BEACH
Racing Association,
CONEY ISLAND,
KINGS COUNTY, N. Y.

OFFICERS FOR 1883.

ROBERT ROBINSON, President.

JAMES McGOWAN, Sec. WILLIAM A. ENGEMAN, Treas.

Executive Committee.

	CHARLES J. FOSTER.	
D. J. McKINLAY.	W. H. STILLWELL.	S. D. HOAGLAND.
W. A. ENGEMAN.	WILL S. RYAN.	JAMES McGOWAN.

Governors.

FELIX CAMPBELL.	HON. A. M. BLISS.	S. H. HARRIMAN.
HUGH McLOUGHLIN.	H. H. WHEELER.	JAMES N. SMITH.
WM. C. KINGSLEY.	WM. MARSHALL.	BENJAMIN LEWIS.
DOMINICK H. ROCHE.	ALBERT DAGGETT.	WM. F. HOWE.
CORNELIUS FERGUSON.	PHILLIP DWYER.	WM. COLE.
	A. BURNHAM.	HENRY C. PLACE.

JAMES McGOWAN, Clerk of the Course. JAMES CLARE, Starter.

Oriental Hotel, Manhattan Beach, Coney Island.

www.ingramcontent.com/pod-product-compliance
Lightning Source LLC
Chambersburg PA
CBHW020257090426
42735CB00009B/1123